The
"I CAN'T BELIEVE
THIS HAS NO SUGAR"
Cookbook, Revised Edition

The "I CAN'T BELIEVE THIS HAS NO SUGAR"

Cookbook, Revised Edition

DEBORAH BUHR

Illustrations by Diana Thewlis

 ST. MARTIN'S GRIFFIN ✖ *New York*

THE "I CAN'T BELIEVE THIS HAS NO SUGAR" COOKBOOK. Copyright © 1990, 1997 by Deborah Buhr. Illustrations copyright © 1990 by Diana Thewlis. All rights reserved. Printed in the United States of America. No part of this book may be used or reproduced in any manner whatsoever without written permission except in the case of brief quotations embodied in critical articles or reviews. For information, address St. Martin's Press, 175 Fifth Avenue, New York, N.Y. 10010.

Library of Congress Cataloging-in-Publication Data

Buhr, Deborah E.
    The "I can't believe this has no sugar" cookbook / Deborah Buhr;
illustrations by Diana Thewlis.—Rev. ed.
        p.   cm.
    Includes bibliographical references and index.
    ISBN 0-312-15551-4
    1. Sugar-free diet—Recipes.   I. Title
RM237.85.B84   1997
641.5'638—dc21   89-54846
                                                            CIP

10   9   8   7   6   5   4

First St. Martin's Griffin Edition: June 1997

For Tara and Michael

CONTENTS

PREFACE

Good-tasting, allergen-free recipes can be very important to patients and families requiring special diets. Deborah Buhr, who, along with her family, has been faced with a variety of food allergies, knows the importance of being able to prepare foods that look like and taste like "the real thing." Fortunately, Deborah has the ability and patience to develop recipes for herself and her family, and I am very pleased that they will now be available to all people with allergies requiring dietary restrictions. These recipes will help them to avoid the most common food allergens: eggs, milk, wheat, corn, and yeast. The recipes are healthy in other ways as well, in that they contain no sugar, honey, or artificial sweeteners and are very low in cholesterol and salt. With this collection of imaginative breads and desserts, I feel that Deborah has given those on restricted diets some latitude in their food choices and options, presenting a variety of foods that can be eaten even though the basic ingredients are controlled. I highly recommend it to the health-conscious, the diabetic, and those prone to food allergy.

—David L. Morris, M.D.
Allergy Associates of La Crosse
Allergy-Immunology
La Crosse, Wisconsin

APPRECIATION

A special thank-you to all the people who helped with the original book, and to my tasting crew for the new recipes. A warm and special thank-you to Barbara and Joy.

INTRODUCTION

"I can't believe this has no sugar." That's what most people say when they taste these recipes. I take this as a great compliment—and as proof that "healthy" food doesn't have to be tasteless or unattractive looking. It can look just as good as commercial products and taste as good, too.

The recipes in this book were developed for people who have allergies to sugarcane, honey, corn syrup, fructose (which contains large amounts of corn), and dairy products (I have provided alternatives for those people who can have dairy), but they will appeal to other health-conscious people as well because of the following:

- These recipes use all natural ingredients—no preservatives, additives, or artificial sweeteners.
- These prepared foods do not cause the "fast rush" associated with foods made with refined sugar (especially important to diabetics).
- The recipes that call for fruit add beneficial fiber, vitamins, and minerals to the diet (there is no fiber in fruit juice concentrates).
- Most of these recipes are lower in calories than the same recipes prepared with cane sugar.
- Fresh fruit and fruit sweeteners are easy to use and add a wide variety of flavors to cakes, pies, and every type of dessert. Once you become accustomed to the subtle, sweet taste of natural fruit, regular desserts will seem cloying and oversweet by comparison.

It is often the case that only one person in a family has special dietary requirements, making it difficult for the "chief cook" to prepare foods that the whole family can enjoy. This is especially true when it comes to desserts. One part of the family demands the appearance and flavor of traditional cakes and cookies and pies; another part of the family requires something quite different and may feel relegated to a life of plain fruit salad for dessert. Fruit sweeteners are the answer to the entire family's needs.

While taking into account the special needs of the diabetic, the hypoglycemic, the overweight, the allergic, the sugar sensitive, and the health-conscious, these recipes provide the great tastes and textures that the whole family wants. Perhaps more important, they allow the person with dietary restrictions to eat foods that *look like* the foods that "other people" eat. In developing these recipes for my family and friends, the appearance of the final product was just as important as the flavor. If it didn't look just like a comparable commercial product or homemade sugar-based product, I didn't feel any pride in serving it or much joy in consuming it. From experience I know how important it is for a person on a special diet to feel "normal" and to feel as if he's eating the same foods as everyone else. When someone eats one of my desserts and says, "I can't believe this has no sugar," I know he's as surprised by the taste as by how it looks. No cook can receive a better compliment—and I hope it's one you'll hear again and again as you prepare the recipes in this book.

COOKING TIPS AND ADVICE ON INGREDIENTS AND SUBSTITUTIONS

Cooking without sugar is not difficult, but it does require careful measurements, the right ingredients, and a few special techniques. The following sections should help you become a pro in the sugar-free kitchen.

COOKING TIPS FOR SUGAR-FREE BAKING

- Use only *unsweetened* frozen fruit juice concentrates. Make sure these do not contain sugar or corn syrup.
- The fruit juice concentrates used in these recipes include Minute Maid reduced-acid orange; any brand of purple grape juice concentrate; white grape juice concentrate; any brand of apple juice concentrate; and black cherry juice concentrate (available at health-food stores, not frozen, in glass bottles). Some of the brand names I have used include:
    Apple: Old Orchard, Adams, Seneca, Minute Maid
    Purple grape: Welch's, Old Orchard
    White grape: Welch's

Black cherry juice concentrate: K. W. Knudsen Family, Tree of Life

Orange reduced-acid: Minute Maid

- When using frozen fruit juice concentrates, do not thaw; rather, measure out what is needed, adding a little at a time to the egg-and-oil mixture, stirring well before adding more. In this way you will avoid having frozen eggs. The remaining concentrate can be returned to the freezer in a plastic bag, to be used later.

- When cooking with fruit concentrates, always combine all ingredients well, then quickly stir in baking soda and baking powder, mix (28 to 30 beats so ingredients are mixed well), *and immediately put the product in the pan and the pan in the oven.* If the baking soda or baking powder is allowed to sit in the fruit mixture, the product won't rise properly.

- If you are allergic to wheat, look for the recipes in this book that call for oat, barley, teff, spelt, amaranth, brown rice, tapioca, or potato flour. Commercial oat and barley flours are available in most health-food stores (Arrowhead Mills is one brand that I recommend), or you may make your own. To make oat flour, place a quantity of Quick Quaker Oats in a blender and mix on high speed for about two minutes, or until oats are very fine. You may occasionally use a teaspoon or knife to push the oat buildup on the sides back to the bottom of the blender. Store leftover flour in a plastic bag. Barley flour can be made in a similar fashion using Quick Quaker Barley (pearled).

  Another oat flour used in these recipes is Wheat-Free Oat Mix by Ener-G, consisting of oat flour and corn-free baking powder. This is available at health-food stores. Teff flour comes in a box and is made by Arrowhead Mills. Spelt flour (Purity Foods, Inc. or Arrowhead Mills), potato flour, tapioca starch flour, amaranth flour (Arrowhead Mills), and brown rice flours are also available at health-food stores.

- If you have celiac disease, be aware that amaranth, potato, brown rice, and tapioca flours do not have gluten. The other flours do.

- Measure correctly and you will be pleased with the results. When measuring flour, always tap the top of the measuring cup two or three times with a knife before leveling it off. If a recipe calls for tapping the flour four to five times, this means the flour should be tapped a little more than usual.

When a liquid measurement calls for a "generous" measure, this means you should fill the measuring utensil to the surface-tension point, that is to the point where adding more liquid will cause the utensil to overflow. A normal liquid measure would be level with the brim. A "generous" dry measure is a rounded measure; a "scant" dry measure means the measuring utensil will be barely full.

- Read each recipe thoroughly in advance, and make sure all the ingredients are ready (i.e., chopped, diced, etc.) before you start.
- Each recipe gives directions for storage after baking. You may freeze portions of the food you do not plan on consuming within three days.

INFORMATION ON INGREDIENTS AND SUBSTITUTIONS

- If you're watching your cholesterol intake, you may substitute two egg whites for each whole egg called for in a recipe. Exceptions are four celiac recipes that are "gluten-free."
- If you are allergic to corn, be aware that most commercial baking powder has a corn base. The recipes in this book were created using commercial baking powder. Corn-free baking powder (made with a potato base) is available at most health-food stores (under the brand name Featherweight Baking Powder), or you can make your own with the following recipe:

Homemade Baking Powder

1 teaspoon baking soda
2 teaspoons arrowroot
2 teaspoons cream of tartar

Mix all ingredients well and store in an airtight container.

Yield: 5 teaspoons

Note: If a recipe calls for 1 teaspoon regular baking powder, substitute 1½ to 1¾ teaspoons homemade baking powder.

- If you are allergic to dairy products, try substituting an equal amount of soy milk (available in many supermarkets and most health-food stores) for milk in any recipe in this book. You can make your own soy milk by mixing soy powder (available in most health-food stores under the brand name Soyquick) with water according to the package directions.

  Another alternative to milk is Rice Dream Original 1% Fat Non-Dairy Beverage made from organic brown rice, filtered water, safflower oil, and sea salt. It's made by Imagine Foods, Inc. *I would not recommend baking with it in these recipes.* It comes in different flavors. You can use it on hot and cold cereals and over hot cooked brown rice with a little cinnamon added. Imagine Foods, Inc., also puts out a Non-Dairy Rice Ice Cream that comes in many flavors, and is sugar-free.

  For an alternative to regular shortening in recipes, try Crisco butter-flavored all-vegetable shortening. It's dairy-free and contains no caseinate, casein, or whey proteins.

- If you are allergic to phenol, an acidic compound used in the lining of many canned goods, use Dole unsweetened pineapple in recipes that call for pineapple slices. Dole does not use phenol in the lining of its cans for pineapple slices in unsweetened juice.

- If you wish to avoid additives and preservatives or sugar and honey, you may want to purchase the following at a health-food store:

date sugar	taro chips
unroasted nuts and seeds	brown and wild rice
brown-rice syrup	vegetables and fruits
unsweetened coconut	cold and hot cereals
dried figs, dates, and raisins	egg replacers

teff whole-grain granules

potato starch flour

potato mix

tapioca starch flour

guar gum

amaranth, spelt, and potato flour

brown-rice-flour

pasta made from wheat, spelt, corn, or rice

Rice Dream (nondairy beverage)

soy milk

rice cakes, corn chips

black cherry juice concentrate

cherry flavoring

canned beans with no additives

- There are two types of flaked coconut: sweetened (available in most supermarkets) and unsweetened (available in health-food stores). Sweetened coconut is moist; unsweetened coconut is not. If you want to use unsweetened coconut you will need to add moisture in the following proportion: For every ½ cup unsweetened coconut, add 1½ teaspoons vegetable oil (I recommend cold-pressed safflower or canola oil, but any oil except olive oil will work) and 1½ teaspoons water. Stir well and let sit for 10 minutes until liquids are absorbed. Use this formula unless directed otherwise in certain recipes. In recipes that call for *dry* coconut, the coconut will absorb moisture from the fruit it's in, so do not premoisten the coconut in these recipes.

- A few recipes call for date sugar, a sweetener made from dehydrated, ground dates. It resembles coarse brown sugar but is not refined and contains valuable minerals and fiber. Date sugar adds a special flavor to Chocolate-Date Cake (page 54) and Cinnamon-Spice Bread (page 13). It is available at most health-food stores.

- Use Minute Tapioca to thicken fruit puddings, pies, and crisps. It will not affect the taste of the fruit.

- Spelt whole-grain flour is becoming popular. It works well in baking, producing great-tasting products. Spelt is a member of the grass family, along with wheat, oats, and barley, and it contains gluten. Spelt has a nutty, mild, pleasant flavor that is similar in taste to whole wheat.

    Spelt has high nutritional value. It's higher in B vitamins and fiber than ordinary bread wheats and has larger amounts of both simple and complex carbohydrates, proteins, and several amino acids. It also contains trace elements and minerals, and is rich in potassium and iron. As dietary fiber goes, ¼ cup of spelt whole-grain flour has 2 grams of fiber.

It is produced organically by Purity Foods, Inc. (Okemos, MI) and Arrowhead Mills, Inc. (Texas). The current product line of Purity Foods, Inc., includes nine types of spelt pasta (made from whole-grain spelt flour), whole-grain and white flours, a pancake-and-muffin mix, and mixes for bread machines. Current products from Arrowhead Mills, Inc., include whole-grain spelt flour, a bread-machine mix for home use, and a flaked (ready-to-eat cold) cereal called Spelt Flakes. These may be purchased at health-food stores.

The Berlin Natural Bakery in Berlin, Ohio, sells five different breads, as well as buns for hamburgers and hot dogs, all made with spelt flour milled at the bakery. Fresh and frozen products from the bakery are shipped daily to states around Ohio.

I've tried baking with spelt whole-grain flour in a few of these recipes; Super-Sweet Blueberry Muffins (page 6), Chocolate-Date Cake (page 54), Cinnamon-Spice Bread (page 13), and Chocolate-Date Cookies (page 162). I found no difference in measurement of all-purpose flour to spelt whole-grain flour. The products tasted fine! When I did make Tara's Sugar-Free White Bread (page 33) recipe with spelt whole-grain flour I needed to add ¼ cup more flour to the kneading of the dough. I also noticed that the first and second rising times were a little faster. The bread was nice and soft, and tasted like whole-wheat bread. My taste testers really enjoyed it! To make things easier for you, I've included the recipe, Spelt Whole-Grain Yeast Bread (see page 41). I haven't tried the spelt white flour, for it's less nutritious, so I don't know whether the measurements would be the same or if you'd have to add more spelt white flour to the recipes. Feel free to experiment!

HOW TO MAKE YOUR OWN FRUIT JUICE CONCENTRATES

You may wish to make your own fruit juice concentrates for several reasons:

- if you cannot find the recommended products in your area (*however, I would not suggest making a pineapple juice concentrate!*)
- if you are allergic to apple
- if commercial fruit juice concentrates contain products that you cannot use
- if you have mold allergies or other allergies that are aggravated by commercial fruit juice concentrates.

Fruit juice concentrates may be made from either purchased fruit juice (watch labels for additives, etc.) *or* from fresh fruit processed with a juicer. The freshest possible juice is provided by a juicer, of which there are four basic types: the hydraulic press, the centrifugal, the pulp-ejection, and the total juicer. Make sure the juicer is made of noncorroding, acid-and alkali-resistant materials, and follow manufacturer's instructions.

You may make your own fruit juice concentrates from fresh fruit such as apple, pear, and grape.

Place 1 quart (4 cups) fruit juice in a heavy saucepan (so juice will not burn) and heat mixture over medium-high heat until juice comes to a boil. Reduce heat, maintaining a slow boil and stirring occasionally, until the 4 cups fruit juice are reduced to 1 cup fruit juice concentrate. More attention is needed in stirring the mixture as the liquid level is reduced. If the concentrate is reduced to less than one cup, add enough water to bring measurement back to one cup.

Cool fruit juice concentrate, place in an airtight container, and freeze. Substitute homemade fruit juice concentrate for those recommended in the recipes.

Yield: 1 cup fresh fruit juice concentrate

A NOTE ON THE NUTRITIONAL ANALYSIS CHARTS

At the end of each recipe, you will find important nutrition information: the calorie count of each serving; the amount, in grams, of protein, fat, carbohydrate, and sodium; and the diabetic exchanges. The nutritional analysis was performed by Marcia Viers, a registered dietitian and certified nutritionist, and by Leslie Weiner and Melanie Polk, also registered dietitians. It is based on the Nutritionist II computer program produced by N-Squared Computing, and on the Food Processor produced by ESHA Research, with input of product nutrient information from various brand-name companies mentioned in the book. The diabetic exchanges were computed by using the Exchange Lists for Meal Planning, a guide updated in 1995 by the American Dietetic Association and the American Diabetes Association.

In using the nutritional analysis charts, you should be aware of the following:

- Nutritional values may vary from brand to brand and will vary depending on the size and ripeness of individual fruits. Thus the nutrient charts in this book should be used as guidelines only, and not as exact measurements.
- Any ingredient listed as "optional" has *not* been calculated into the nutritional breakdown. If you choose to add optional ingredients, be aware that nuts, seeds, and coconut will add substantially to the readings, especially those for calories and fat.
- Whenever two or more choices are given in the ingredient list (for example, "4 egg whites *or* 2 whole eggs"), only the first option has been calculated into the nutritional breakdown. If you use one of the alternate ingredients instead of the first-mentioned ingredient, be aware that the nutritional breakdown of the recipe will change. For example, using whole eggs instead of egg whites will add cholesterol to the recipe; using butter or lard instead of vegetable oil will add more saturated fat and will introduce cholesterol into the recipe.
- Whenever a range of measurement is given for a certain ingredient or whenever a range of serving sizes is given, the first measurement or size is the one used to calculate the nutritional breakdown.
- Only the main recipes, not the variations, have been analyzed.
- The recipes in the chapter on fresh fruits have not been analyzed. Instead, on pages 174–177, you will find nutritional breakdowns for a wide variety of fresh fruits, fruit juices, and fruit concentrates. These charts can be used to calculate the nutrients in the various recipes.
- Calorie counts and diabetic exchanges may look high compared to those found in other cookbooks, but portion sizes in this book are quite generous and, we feel, more realistic than those provided in other books.

The
"I CAN'T BELIEVE
THIS HAS NO SUGAR"
Cookbook, Revised Edition

QUICK BREADS AND YEAST BREADS

Including Muffins, Pizza Crusts, and Rolls

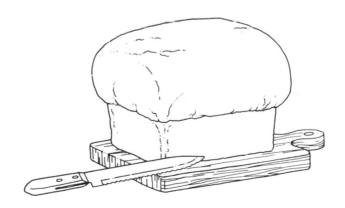

Breads made with natural fruit sweeteners are easy to prepare and can be served at any meal. Slice and toast them for breakfast, spread with sugar-free jam or butter. Try them as the base for your favorite sandwich filling at lunch. Send muffins or individual slices of bread to school with your children or serve them with afternoon tea. At dinnertime, try them with soups, or topped with fresh fruit, pudding, or whipped cream for an elegant dessert.

If you have experience in baking fresh yeast bread from scratch, these sugar-free yeast breads will be a breeze. The mixing, rising, and baking processes are the same as for regular bread, and the "feel" of the dough at each stage will be the same, too. If you are new to bread baking, you'll find that it really is easy. Just be sure to follow the directions closely and to be aware of the feel of the dough.

Realize that the quantity of flour needed to bring the dough to the right consistency depends on many things—the type of flour, the humidity, even the temperature of the air and of your hands—so don't be surprised if you have to use a little more or less flour than called for in a recipe. The important thing is to go by how the dough feels to the touch. Any doubts you have about your abilities as a bread baker will be dispelled by the aroma and taste of your own freshly baked bread. Once you and your family try it, you'll be hooked!

Here are a few hints to get you started:

- Use only the freshest yeast. Fresh yeast will *bubble* when mixed with warm water, fruit concentrate, and a few teaspoons of flour. If your yeast doesn't bubble, throw it out and start with a new batch; otherwise, you may spend the next three hours making bread that won't rise properly.

- Measure all ingredients carefully. Add flour gradually until the dough reaches the consistency called for in the recipe.
- When a recipe says to *knead the dough in the pan, do not* take the dough out of the pan and knead it on a floured surface. Leave the dough in the pan and add the flour. The recipe will tell you for how long a period you have to add flour and knead. Dough should be soft but not sticky to the touch. For the first rising period, simply cover pan and let dough rise.
- When a recipe says to *knead the dough on a floured surface,* transfer the dough from the pan to a lightly floured surface and knead, adding more flour as needed, for the amount of time indicated. Dough should be soft but not sticky to the touch.
- When a recipe instructs you to knead the dough for one minute after the first rising period and before making loaf or rolls, take the cover off the pan that the dough was rising in, and knead dough for one minute *in pan. Do not* add flour. What you are doing is moving the fruit sugar around so that the yeast has a new food source.
- Knead fruit-sweetened dough as if it were regular sugar-sweetened dough. When the dough is soft and silky smooth to the touch and not sticky, it is ready for the first rising period. Sometimes the dough will feel rubbery at this stage and the dough will shine. This stage is usually reached after you've been kneading for several minutes without having to add extra flour.
- If a recipe calls for coating the dough with oil, do it gently, with your fingertips.
- Check the dough periodically during the rising period to make sure it doesn't rise too long. With traditional dough, the yeast uses sugar as a food during the rising period. Since you are using natural fruit sugars instead of refined sugar, the yeast will run out of food a little sooner and will start to deflate. To avoid this, set a timer at the start of each rising period and check the dough five to ten minutes before the end of the stated rising time. If the dough looks as though it has doubled in bulk, proceed to punch it down and follow the next step of the recipe's directions.

- As you shape the loaf before the second rising period, treat the dough gently, as though you were working with something fragile, and be sure to roll out the dough to the correct thickness. If you roll out the dough too thin, it will not make a beautiful loaf; if you are too rough with the dough, the same thing will happen.

- After you put the shaped dough in the baking pan(s), you can determine when it is ready for the oven by its size and appearance. The dough will likely have risen two inches above the sides of the pan, and it will appear to have "little windows" as the gluten is activated and forms strands in the dough. You can see this especially clearly on cinnamon rolls. When the dough reaches this stage, put it in the oven and bake it as soon as possible; otherwise, it may deflate like a pricked balloon.

- If you use your oven as the rising place, remember that it takes seven to ten minutes to get the oven to 350°F, so calculate that time into your rising time and remove the dough from the oven a little before it has risen completely.

- When bread is done, it will be slightly golden on top and will sound hollow when tapped lightly with your fingertips or a knife. When the bread has this hollow sound, remove it from the oven, tap the bread out of the pan (bread will slide out of the pan easily when it's done), and place it on a wire rack to cool.

- Remember that one whole egg or two egg whites may be used interchangeably in these bread recipes.

- Read each recipe thoroughly in advance and make sure all the ingredients are ready before you start.

Banana-Blueberry Muffins

1 cup mashed banana
2 egg whites *or* 1 extralarge egg
½ cup water
⅓ cup vegetable oil
2 cups all-purpose flour

1 teaspoon baking soda
2¼ teaspoons baking powder
1 cup fresh or frozen blueberries, left to
  thaw in a strainer

1. Preheat oven to 350°F. Prepare 18 standard-sized muffin cups with paper liners.

2. In a large bowl, stir together banana, egg, water, and oil. Add flour and mix. Stir in baking soda and baking powder quickly, and then mix (28 to 30 beats). Gently fold in blueberries. Immediately spoon batter into prepared muffin cups.

3. Bake about 20 minutes, or until a cake tester inserted in the center of one muffin comes out clean. As soon as they are done, remove muffins from tins and cool on a wire rack. Serve warm or cool completely and store in an airtight container on countertop or freeze.

Yield: 18 muffins

PER MUFFIN

Calories: 105
Protein: 2.0 g
Fat: 4.2 g
Carbohydrate: 14.8 g

Sodium: 93 mg
Diabetic exchanges
  Starch: 1
  Fat: ¾

Super-Sweet Blueberry Muffins

1 cup mashed banana
2 egg whites *or* 1 extralarge egg
⅓ cup vegetable oil
½ cup unsweetened apple juice
   concentrate (any brand)
1 tablespoon water
2 cups all-purpose flour
1 cup fresh or frozen blueberries, left to
   thaw in a strainer
2 teaspoons baking soda

1. Preheat oven to 350°F. Prepare 18 standard-sized muffin cups with paper liners.

2. In a large bowl, stir together banana, egg, oil, concentrate, and water. Add flour and mix. Gently stir in blueberries. Stir in baking soda quickly, and then mix (28 to 30 beats). Immediately spoon batter into prepared muffin cups.

3. Bake about 20 minutes, or until a cake tester inserted in the center of one muffin comes out clean. As soon as they are done, remove muffins from tins and cool on a wire rack. Serve warm or cool completely and store in an airtight container on countertop or freeze.

Yield: 18 muffins

PER MUFFIN

Calories: 117
Protein: 2 g
Fat: 4.3 g
Carbohydrate: 17.9 g

Sodium: 148.8 mg
Diabetic exchanges
  Starch: 1
  Fat: 1

Cinnamon-Spice Muffins

1½ cups all-purpose flour, tapped lightly 4 or 5 times

½ cup plus 3 tablespoons packed date sugar

Scant 1½ teaspoons cinnamon

3 to 4 dashes nutmeg

Generous ½ cup vegetable oil

⅓ cup plus 1 tablespoon zucchini pulp (puree zucchini in blender or food processor with a little water; drain out liquid with hand strainer)

⅓ cup plus 1 tablespoon unsweetened apple juice concentrate (any brand)

Generous 2 tablespoons water

4 egg whites *or* 2 extralarge eggs, beaten

Generous 1½ teaspoons baking soda

1. Preheat oven to 325°F. Prepare 15 standard-sized muffin cups with paper liners.

2. In a large bowl, stir together flour, date sugar, cinnamon, nutmeg, oil, pureed zucchini, and concentrate.

3. Add water and eggs and stir for 2 to 3 minutes by hand. Stir in baking soda quickly, and then mix (28 to 30 beats). Immediately spoon batter into prepared muffin cups.

4. Bake 18 to 20 minutes, or until a cake tester inserted in the center of one muffin comes out clean. As soon as they are done, remove muffins from tins and cool on a wire rack. Serve warm or cool completely and store in an airtight container on countertop or freeze.

Yield: 15 muffins

PER MUFFIN

Calories: 149.5　　*Sodium:* 142.7 mg
Protein: 2.3 g　　*Diabetic exchanges*
Fat: 7.4 g　　　　*Starch:* 1
Carbohydrate: 18.4 g　　*Fat:* 1½

Apple-Banana Muffins

Generous ¾ cup mashed banana

4 egg whites *or* 2 extralarge eggs

⅓ cup vegetable oil

½ cup unsweetened apple juice
   concentrate (any brand)

1 tablespoon plus 1 teaspoon water

2 cups all-purpose flour

¾ teaspoon cinnamon

⅓ cup chopped walnuts

2 teaspoons baking soda

1. Preheat oven to 350°F. Prepare 18 or 19 standard-sized muffin cups with paper liners.

2. In a large bowl, stir together banana, eggs, oil, concentrate, and water. Add flour, cinnamon, and nuts; mix well for 1 to 2 minutes. Stir in baking soda quickly, and then mix (28 to 30 beats). Immediately spoon batter into prepared muffin cups.

3. Bake about 18 minutes, or until a cake tester inserted in the center of one muffin comes out clean. As soon as they are done, remove muffins from tins and cool on a wire rack. Serve warm or cool completely and store in an airtight container on countertop or freeze.

Yield: 18 or 19 muffins

PER MUFFIN

Calories: 125.7

Protein: 2.9 g

Fat: 5.5 g

Carbohydrate: 16.4 g

Sodium: 154.4 mg

Diabetic exchanges

   Starch: 1

   Fat: 1

Egg Muffins

Gluten-Free
Contains Egg Yolks; Not Cholesterol-Free

½ cup tapioca starch flour, packed
4 extralarge eggs
¼ teaspoon salt

2 tablespoons water
1½ teaspoons homemade baking
    powder

1. Preheat oven to 350°F. Oil 17 regular-sized muffin cups. Set aside.
2. Measure flour into a small bowl, stir well with a spoon, and set aside.
3. Separate your eggs, placing yolks in a large-sized bowl, whites in a medium-sized bowl. Using a hand-operated mechanical beater, beat egg whites until very stiff. They should not fall out of the bowl when the bowl is turned upside down. Set whites aside.
4. Using a hand-operated mechanical beater, beat egg yolks. Add salt, water, and flour and stir well. Rebeat egg whites to make sure they are stiff. Quickly add baking powder to yolk mixture and mix well. Fold in stiff egg whites.
5. Quickly spoon batter into prepared muffin cups. Bake for 15 minutes, or until a cake tester inserted in center of muffin comes out clean.
6. Remove tins from oven and, using a knife, cut around sides of muffins and pop muffins out of cups with a spoon. Place lightly into a serving basket. Serve warm. Leftover muffins can be frozen in a plastic bag.

Yield: 17 muffins

PER MUFFIN

Calories: 32.7
Protein: 1.7 g
Fat: 1.4 g
Carbohydrate: 3.2 g

Sodium: 48.5 mg
Diabetic exchanges
  Starch: ½

Banana Bread

Generous ¾ cup mashed banana
⅓ cup vegetable oil
4 egg whites *or* 2 extralarge eggs
½ cup water
2 cups all-purpose flour

Scant ½ teaspoon cinnamon
Scant ½ teaspoon nutmeg
1 cup chopped nuts (optional)
Generous 1 teaspoon baking soda
Generous 2¼ teaspoons baking powder

1. Preheat oven to 325°F. Coat a 9- by 5- by 2¾-inch loaf pan with vegetable oil or vegetable shortening.

2. In a large bowl, and using a hand-operated mechanical beater, whip together banana, oil, eggs, and water.

3. Add flour, cinnamon, nutmeg, and nuts, if desired, to banana mixture; mix. Stir in baking soda and baking powder quickly, and then mix (28 to 30 beats). Immediately pour batter into prepared loaf pan.

4. Bake 50 to 53 minutes, or until a knife inserted in the center of the loaf comes out clean. Loosen bread from pan with a knife and turn loaf out onto a wire rack to cool. To store, wrap cooled loaf in plastic and store on countertop or freeze.

Yield: One 9- by 5- by 2¾-inch loaf (12 slices)

PER SLICE

Calories: 143
Protein: 3.1 g
Fat: 6.3 g
Carbohydrate: 18.2 g

Sodium: 147.0 mg
Diabetic exchanges
  Starch: 1¼
  Fat: 1

Apple-Banana Bread

Generous ¾ cup mashed banana
⅓ cup vegetable oil
4 egg whites *or* 2 extralarge eggs
½ cup unsweetened apple juice
    concentrate (any brand)
1 tablespoon plus 1 teaspoon water

2 cups all-purpose flour
Scant ½ teaspoon cinnamon
Scant ½ teaspoon nutmeg
1 cup chopped nuts
2 teaspoons baking soda

1. Preheat oven to 325°F. Coat a 9- by 5- by 2¾-inch loaf pan with vegetable oil or vegetable shortening.

2. In a large bowl, and using a hand-operated mechanical beater, whip together banana, oil, eggs, concentrate, and water.

3. Add flour, cinnamon, nutmeg, and nuts to banana mixture and mix. Stir in baking soda quickly, and then mix (28 to 30 beats). Immediately pour batter into prepared loaf pan.

4. Bake 50 minutes. Make a "tent" of aluminum foil and place it over the entire loaf pan. Bake another 7 to 8 minutes, or until a knife inserted in the center of the loaf comes out clean. Loosen bread from pan with a knife and turn loaf onto a wire rack to cool. To store, wrap cooled loaf in plastic and store on countertop or freeze.

Yield: One 9- by 5- by 2¾-inch loaf (12 slices)

PER SLICE (USING WALNUTS FOR CHOPPED NUTS)

Calories: 231.3
Protein: 6.1 g
Fat: 12.3 g
Carbohydrate: 25.5 g

Sodium: 231.6 mg
Diabetic exchanges
    Starch: 2
    Fat: 2½

Zucchini-Apple Quick Bread

4 egg whites *or* 2 extralarge eggs
Generous ⅓ cup plus 1 teaspoon
  vegetable oil
¾ cup zucchini pulp (puree zucchini in
  blender or food processor with a
  little water; strain out liquid with
  hand strainer)

1¼ cups unsweetened apple juice
  concentrate (any brand)
Generous 1½ teaspoons cinnamon
2¾ cups all-purpose flour, tapped
  lightly 4 to 5 times
2⅜ teaspoons baking soda

1. Preheat oven to 325°F. Coat two 9- by 5- by 2¾-inch loaf pans with vegetable oil or vegetable shortening.

2. In a large bowl, and using a hand-operated mechanical beater, whip together (for 30 seconds) the eggs, oil, pureed zucchini, and concentrate.

3. Add cinnamon and flour to zucchini mixture and beat for 3 minutes by hand. Stir in baking soda quickly, and then mix (28 to 30 beats). Immediately pour batter into prepared loaf pans.

4. Bake 35 to 37 minutes, or until a knife inserted in the center of the loaves comes out clean. Loosen bread from pans with a knife and turn loaves out onto a wire rack to cool. To store, wrap cooled loaves in plastic and store on countertop or freeze.

Yield: Two 9- by 5- by 2¾-inch loaves (20 slices)

PER SLICE

Calories: 130.3
Protein: 2.6 g
Fat: 4.1 g
Carbohydrate: 20.7 g
Sodium: 102.4 mg

Diabetic exchanges
  Starch: 1
  Fat: 1
  Vegetable: 1

Cinnamon-Spice Bread

1½ cups all-purpose flour, tapped lightly 4 to 5 times

½ cup plus 3 tablespoons packed date sugar

Scant 1½ teaspoons cinnamon

3 to 4 dashes nutmeg

Generous ½ cup vegetable oil

⅓ cup plus 1 tablespoon zucchini pulp (puree zucchini in blender or food processor with a little water; strain out liquid with hand strainer)

⅓ cup plus 1 tablespoon unsweetened apple juice concentrate (any brand)

Generous 2 tablespoons water

4 egg whites *or* 2 extralarge eggs, beaten

Generous 1½ teaspoons baking soda

1. Preheat oven to 325°F. Oil or grease a 9- by 5- by 2¾-inch loaf pan with vegetable oil or vegetable shortening.

2. In a large bowl, stir together flour, date sugar, cinnamon, nutmeg, oil, pureed zucchini, and concentrate.

3. Add water and eggs and stir for 2 to 3 minutes by hand. Stir in baking soda quickly, and then mix (28 to 30 beats). Immediately pour batter into prepared loaf pan.

4. Bake 42 to 45 minutes, or until a knife inserted in the center of the loaf comes out clean. Loosen bread from pan with a knife and turn loaf out onto a wire rack to cool. To store, wrap cooled loaf in plastic and store on countertop or freeze.

Yield: One 9- by 5- by 2¾-inch loaf (12 slices)

PER SLICE

Calories: 187
Protein: 2.9 g
Fat: 9.3 g
Carbohydrate: 23.1 g
Sodium: 178.4 mg

Diabetic exchanges
  Starch: 1
  Fat: 2
  Fruit: ½

Waffles

No Egg

¾ cup water
¾ cup plus 2 tablespoons all-purpose
  flour
3 tablespoons vegetable oil
1 tablespoon unsweetened apple juice
  concentrate (any brand)

¼ cup vegetable oil
1 cup water
1 teaspoon salt
2 cups all-purpose flour
4¼ to 4½ teaspoons baking powder

1. Preheat waffle iron.

2. In a large bowl, stir together ¾ cup water, ¾ cup plus 2 tablespoons flour, and 3 tablespoons oil.

3. Add concentrate, ¼ cup oil, 1 cup water, salt, and 2 cups flour. Mix well.

4. Stir in baking powder quickly, and then mix (28 to 30 beats). Pour half the batter into preheated large waffle iron.

5. Cook waffles to desired doneness. Loosen waffles from iron and place waffles on serving platter. Pour rest of batter into hot waffle iron and cook waffles as before (see *Note*).

Yield: 8 waffles

Note: Extra waffles can be cooled on a wire rack, wrapped in aluminum foil, and stored in the freezer. To reheat, place unwrapped frozen waffle in wide toaster and heat.

PER WAFFLE

Calories: 273.9
Protein: 4.6 g
Fat: 12.4 g
Carbohydrate: 35.9 g

Sodium: 527 mg
Diabetic exchanges
  Starch: 2½
  Fat: 2½

Potato Mix Waffles— Cereal-Free

Gluten-Free
Contains Egg Yolks; Not Cholesterol-Free

2 extralarge eggs
¾ cup Ener-G Brand Potato Mix
  (contains corn-free baking
  powder); fill ½ cup and ¼ cup
  generously, press down with side
  of knife, level off
1½ teaspoons unsweetened apple juice
  concentrate (any brand)

½ teaspoon salt
2 tablespoons vegetable oil
½ cup water
2¼ teaspoons Featherweight baking
  powder (cereal-free) or
  homemade baking powder

1. Separate your eggs, placing the egg yolks in a large-sized bowl and the egg whites in a small-sized bowl. Using a hand-operated mechanical beater, beat egg whites until very stiff. They should not fall out of the bowl when the bowl is turned upside down. Set whites aside.

2. Add Potato Mix, concentrate, salt, oil, and water to egg yolks. Mix ingredients well. Rebeat egg whites to make sure they are stiff. Quickly add baking powder to yolk mixture and mix well. Fold in stiff egg whites.

3. Pour half of batter into preheated large waffle iron. Cook waffles until crisp so they will not be doughy inside. Loosen waffles from iron and place on serving platter. Pour rest of batter into hot waffle iron and cook waffles as before (see *Note*).

Yield: 6 waffles

Note: Extra waffles can be cooled on a wire rack, wrapped in aluminum foil, and stored in the freezer. To reheat, place unwrapped frozen waffle in wide toaster and heat.

PER WAFFLE

Calories: 143.7
Protein: 2.8 g
Fat: 6.5 g
Carbohydrate: 18.6 g

Sodium: 254.9 mg
Diabetic exchanges
  Starch: 1
  Fat: 1

Stuffing

This is an old family recipe, German in origin, that has been handed down on my husband's side. The original recipe called for 1 to 2 tablespoons of sugar, which I've omitted. Believe me, it's a great stuffing!

Using a nonbasted 11- to 12- pound bird, thaw turkey for three days or so in refrigerator. Remove covering, remove fat and packaged innards, and clean bird, rinsing well with water.

8 slices bread, laid to dry for 1 day, then cut into 1-inch cubes

4 large apples, peeled, cored, and diced

1 to 1¼ cups raisins

Generous ½ teaspoon cinnamon

1. In a large bowl, combine all ingredients and add a little water to moisten. (Stuffing should not be mushy—just moist enough to pack your bird. Feel it with your hand; if it packs together, do not add more water.)

2. Stuff bird. Remember that stuffing will expand, so leave a little room. Lace or sew turkey closed. If you have extra stuffing that will not fit into the bird, place it in an oiled glass dish, cover, and bake 45 to 50 minutes at 350°F. When done, add turkey drippings as in step 5.

3. Preheat oven to 450°F.

4. Place turkey on a rack in a turkey roaster so the bird does not sit in liquid while it cooks. Season to taste with salt and pepper. Add 2½ cups water to pan. Cover turkey roaster with heavy aluminum foil, sealing edges to keep in moisture. Bake 1 hour at 450° F; turn down oven to 400°F and bake 1 hour; turn down oven to 375°F and bake 1¼ hours; turn down oven to 350°F and bake 45 minutes. During the last 45 minutes, remove aluminum foil from all parts of turkey except legs (and remove foil completely for last 20 minutes of baking time). Baste with turkey drippings every 15 to 20 minutes of last 45 minutes of baking time.

5. Remove turkey from oven. Spoon stuffing from bird and let bird cool 10 minutes before carving. While bird is cooling, add a small amount (about 2 tablespoons) of pan drippings to stuffing. Stir, adding drippings a little at a time until stuffing is just moist. Serve hot.

Yield: Enough stuffing for an 11- to 12- pound bird (12 servings)

PER SERVING (BEFORE ADDING PAN DRIPPINGS)

Calories: 115
Protein: 2.4 g
Fat: 0.9 g
Carbohydrate: 26.5 g

Sodium: 97.6 mg
Diabetic exchanges
Starch: ¾
Fruit: 1

Baking Powder Biscuits

1¾ cups all-purpose flour, tapped
   lightly 4 to 5 times
2½ teaspoons baking powder
¾ teaspoon salt
½ cup plus 1 tablespoon plus 1½
   teaspoons water

1 tablespoon unsweetened apple juice
   concentrate (any brand)
Generous 3 tablespoons vegetable oil

1. Preheat oven to 450°F. Lightly oil a small baking sheet.

2. Measure flour, baking powder, and salt into a medium-sized bowl and sift three times.

3. In another medium-sized bowl, stir together water, concentrate, and oil.

4. Pour concentrate mixture over dry ingredients and stir to mix with a fork.

5. Place dough on a lightly floured surface and knead ten to fifteen times. Add a little more flour if dough is sticky. Pat out dough to 1-inch thickness.

6. Cut dough with biscuit cutter and place on prepared baking sheet. Bake 10 to 12 minutes, or until there is a trace of gold on bottoms, sides, and tops of biscuits. Remove baking sheet from oven and immediately place biscuits in bread basket lined with cloth; cover biscuits to keep them warm. Serve warm or cold. To store, wrap cooled biscuits in plastic and store on countertop.

Yield: 8 biscuits

PER BISCUIT

Calories: 149.1
Protein: 2.9 g
Fat: 5.4 g
Carbohydrate: 22.2 g

Sodium: 353.3 mg
Diabetic exchanges
  Starch: 1½
  Fat: 1

Soy Milk (or Buttermilk) Biscuits

1½ tablespoons soy powder or dry
    buttermilk (see *Note*)
2 cups all-purpose flour
2¼ teaspoons baking powder
1 teaspoon salt
½ teaspoon baking soda

⅓ cup vegetable shortening or lard
3 tablespoons unsweetened apple juice
    concentrate (any brand)
⅓ cup plus 2 tablespoons plus 1
    teaspoon water
Scant 2 teaspoons lemon juice

1. Preheat oven to 425°F.

2. In a medium-sized bowl, combine soy powder (or dry buttermilk), flour, baking powder, salt, and soda. Sift mixture three or four times.

3. Using a pastry cutter, cut shortening into flour mixture until it resembles cornmeal. If you won't be making biscuits immediately, store mixture covered in refrigerator after shortening has been added.

4. Five minutes before you are to put biscuits in oven, in a small bowl combine concentrate, water, and lemon juice. Pour liquid over flour mixture and stir gently just to moisten.

5. Place dough on a lightly floured surface and knead gently twenty times. Flatten dough with your hands to ½- to ¾-inch thickness.

6. Cut dough with biscuit cutter and place on ungreased baking sheet. Bake 10 to 12 minutes, or until there is a trace of gold on bottoms, sides, and tops of biscuits. Remove baking sheet from oven and immediately place biscuits in bread basket lined with cloth; cover biscuits to keep them warm. Serve warm.

Yield: 10 to 11 biscuits

Note: If not using Soyquick, use cultured Buttermilk Blend by Sa Company and use water instead of lemon juice.

PER BISCUIT

Calories: 162.8	*Sodium:* 387.6 mg
Protein: 2.8 g	*Diabetic exchanges*
Fat: 7.2 g	*Starch:* 1½
Carbohydrate: 21.7 g	*Fat:* 1½

Whole-Wheat Biscuits

1¼ cups all-purpose flour, tapped
   lightly 4 to 5 times
½ cup 100% stone-ground whole-
   wheat flour
2½ teaspoons plus ⅛ teaspoon baking
   powder

¾ teaspoon salt
½ cup plus 1 tablespoon water
1 tablespoon unsweetened apple juice
   concentrate (any brand)
3 tablespoons vegetable oil

1. Preheat oven to 450°F. Lightly oil a small baking sheet.

2. Measure flours, baking powder, and salt into a medium-sized bowl and sift three times.

3. In another medium-sized bowl, stir together water, concentrate, and oil.

4. Pour concentrate mixture over dry ingredients and stir with a fork until just blended. Use your hands to mix in flour if using the fork is getting difficult.

5. Place dough on a lightly floured surface (use all-purpose flour) and knead gently 10 to 12 times. Pat out dough to about ¾-inch thickness.

6. Cut dough with biscuit cutter and place on prepared baking sheet. Bake 11 to 12 minutes, or until the bottoms, sides, and tops of biscuits are lightly golden. Remove baking sheet from oven and immediately place biscuits in bread basket lined with cloth; cover biscuits to keep them warm. Serve warm or cold. To store, wrap cooled biscuits in plastic and store on countertop or freeze.

Yield: 8 biscuits

PER BISCUIT

Calories: 146.1
Protein: 3.1 g
Fat: 5.5 g
Carbohydrate: 21.7 g

Sodium: 361.2 mg
Diabetic exchanges
  Starch: 1½
  Fat: 1

Spelt Whole-Grain Soda Drop Biscuits

Has Gluten

2 cups spelt whole-grain flour, tapped
    lightly 4 to 5 times
Scant ½ teaspoon salt

1¼ teaspoons baking soda
1¼ teaspoons cream of tartar
1 cup water

1. Preheat oven to 425°F. Lightly oil a large baking sheet.

2. Measure flour, salt, baking soda, and cream of tartar into a medium-sized bowl and mix will with a spoon.

3. Add water and stir until just blended.

4. Drop batter by heaping spoonfuls into twelve portions onto baking sheet.

5. Bake 14 to 15 minutes, or until lightly browned. Remove baking sheet from oven and immediately place biscuits in bread basket lined with cloth; cover biscuits to keep them warm. Serve warm or cold. To store, wrap cooled biscuits in plastic and store on countertop or freeze.

Yield: 12 biscuits

PER BISCUIT

Calories: 74.2
Protein: 3.3 g
Fat: 0.7 g
Carbohydrate: 15.6 g

Sodium: 220.1 mg
Diabetic exchanges
   Starch: 1

Biscuits with Dried Fruit and Cinnamon

Dough

1¾ cups all-purpose flour, tapped lightly 4 to 5 times

2½ teaspoons baking powder

¾ teaspoon salt

½ cup plus 1 tablespoon plus 1½ teaspoons water

1 tablespoon unsweetened apple juice concentrate (any brand)

Generous 3 tablespoons vegetable oil

FILLING

17 dried dates cut up with scissors into small pieces or ¾ cup raisins

Cinnamon to taste

1. Preheat oven to 400°F. Lightly oil a small baking sheet. Prepare filling ingredients.

2. Measure flour, baking powder, and salt into a medium-sized bowl and sift three times.

3. In another medium-sized bowl, stir together water, concentrate, and oil.

4. Pour concentrate mixture over dry ingredients and stir to mix with a fork.

5. Place dough on a lightly floured surface and knead 10 to 13 times. Add a little more flour if dough is sticky. On a lightly floured surface, roll out the dough to form a rectangle with a generous ½-inch thickness.

6. Sprinkle dough with cinnamon and place date pieces or raisins all over top of dough. Roll up jelly roll style and cut into eight 1-inch to 1¼-inch pieces. Place biscuits on baking sheet and sprinkle cinnamon over tops.

7. Bake for 15 to 16 minutes or so. Biscuits should not feel rubbery when done. Remove baking sheet from oven and immediately place biscuits on a wire rack to cool. Serve warm or cold. To store, wrap cooled biscuits in plastic and store on countertop or freeze.

Yield: 8 biscuits

Calories: 197.8
Protein: 3.2 g
Fat: 5.5 g
Carbohydrates: 35.2 g
Sodium: 353.9 mg

Diabetic exchanges
 Starch: 1
 Fat: 1
 Fruit: 1½

Cloverleaf Rolls

Knead in Pan

8 cups all-purpose flour

2 packages yeast

2 teaspoons all-purpose flour

½ cup unsweetened apple juice
concentrate (any brand)

¼ cup water

1¾ cups water, milk, or soy milk

½ cup vegetable shortening or lard

2 teaspoons salt

4 egg whites *or* 2 extralarge eggs,
beaten

2 to 3 tablespoons olive oil or oil of
choice

1. Measure 8 cups flour into a large bowl and sift four times.

2. In a small bowl, stir together yeast and 2 teaspoons flour.

3. Place concentrate and ¼ cup water in a small saucepan and warm to 120°F. Pour over flour-and-yeast mixture, stir gently to moisten, and let stand for 10 minutes.

4. In a 4-quart or larger saucepan or pot, combine 1¾ cups water (or milk or soy milk), shortening, and salt. Heat mixture to 130°F, remove pan from heat, and let cool to 120°F.

5. Add 2 cups sifted flour to water-and-shortening mixture and stir to count of 20. Add yeast mixture and stir to count of 20. Add 1 cup sifted flour and stir to count of 20. Add eggs and stir to count of 20.

6. Start timing: Knead for 10 minutes in the pan, *not on a floured surface*, gradually adding flour until the dough is soft and not sticky to the touch (you may not need to use all the sifted flour). Make sure you work the dough until it is smooth and elastic. Leave dough in pan, cover with a towel, and let rise in a warm place for 40 to 45 minutes.

7. Generously coat 30 muffin cups with vegetable oil or shortening.

8. Punch down dough, leave *in pan*, and knead for 1 minute. *Do not* add flour.

9. Roll small portions of dough in the palms of your hands to create ninety 1-inch balls. Place 3 balls in each prepared muffin cup. Cover tins with a towel and let rise in a warm place for 45 minutes.

10. Preheat oven to 375°F.

11. Bake about 17 minutes, or until lightly golden. Remove tins from oven and turn out rolls onto a wire rack to cool. Using a brush, cover tops of rolls with olive oil (or oil of choice). Serve warm or wrap cooled rolls in plastic and store on countertop or freeze.

Yield: 30 muffin-size rolls

PER CLOVERLEAF ROLL

Calories: 171.5   *Sodium:* 151.5 mg
Protein: 4.1 g   *Diabetic exchanges*
Fat: 4.7 g   *Bread:* 1½
Carbohydrate: 27.7 g   *Fat:* 1

Apple-Cinnamon or Pear-Cinnamon Rolls

Knead in Pan

8 cups all-purpose flour
2 packages yeast
2 teaspoons all-purpose flour
¼ cup unsweetened apple juice
   concentrate (any brand)
½ cup water

1¾ cups water, milk, or soy milk
½ cup vegetable shortening, vegetable
   oil, *or* lard
1 teaspoon salt
4 egg whites *or* 2 extralarge eggs,
   beaten

FILLING

5 tablespoons vegetable shortening,
   vegetable oil, or lard

1½ to 1¾ teaspoons cinnamon
3¾ cups chopped fruit of choice

1. Measure 8 cups flour into a large bowl and sift four times.

2. In a small bowl, stir together yeast and 2 teaspoons flour.

3. Place concentrate and ½ cup water in a small saucepan; warm to 120°F. Pour over flour-and-yeast mixture, stir gently to moisten, and let stand for 10 minutes.

4. In a 4-quart or larger saucepan or pot, combine 1¾ cups water (or milk or soy milk), shortening, and salt. Heat mixture to 130°F; remove from heat and let cool to 120°F.

5. Add 2 cups of the sifted flour to water-and-shortening mixture and stir to count of 20. Add yeast mixture and stir to count of 20. Add eggs and stir to count of 20. Add 1 cup sifted flour and stir to count of 20.

6. Start timing: Knead for 10 minutes in the pan, *not on a floured surface*, gradually adding flour until the dough is soft and not sticky to the touch (you may not need to use all the sifted flour). Make sure you work the dough until it is smooth and elastic. Leave dough in pan, cover with a towel, and let rise in a warm place for 40 to 45 minutes. While dough is rising, make filling.

7. *To prepare filling:* Place shortening, cinnamon, and chopped fruit in a small saucepan and heat until shortening is melted. Remove from heat and cool. Divide filling into three portions.

8. Generously coat three 9- by 9- by 2-inch pans with vegetable oil or vegetable shortening.

9. Punch down dough, leave in pan, and knead for 1 minute. *Do not* add flour. Divide dough into three portions. Roll out each portion on a lightly floured surface to ½-inch thickness. Spread filling on dough. Roll up each portion of dough and filling; cut each into nine 1½-inch pieces (27 pieces total).

10. Place 9 rolls in each pan. Cover pans with towels and let rise in a warm place for 50 minutes.

11. Preheat oven to 350°F.

12. Bake about 25 minutes, or until sides and tops are *slightly* golden. Remove pans from oven, turn out rolls onto a plate, cover with another plate, and turn over. Top rolls, while warm, with butter, Apple Drizzle Topping (page 27), another topping of your choice, or eat plain. Serve warm or cool completely, wrap in plastic, and refrigerate or freeze. Total preparation time is approximately 3½ hours.

Yield: 27 rolls

PER ROLL (USING APPLES AS FRUIT OF CHOICE IN FILLING)

Calories: 207.4   *Diabetic exchanges*
Protein: 4.6 g   *Starch:* 1
Fat: 6.6 g   *Fat:* 1
Carbohydrate: 32.1 g   *Fruit:* 1
Sodium: 88.8 mg

Apple-Nut Cinnamon Rolls

To make the preparation easier for you, I suggest having the ingredients in step 4 in a saucepan ahead of time, ready to heat.

Knead in Pan

8½ to 9 cups all-purpose flour

2 packages yeast

2 teaspoons all-purpose flour

½ cup unsweetened apple juice concentrate (any brand)

½ cup plus 1 tablespoon water

1½ cups unsweetened apple juice concentrate (any brand)

½ cup plus 2 tablespoons water

½ cup plus 1½ teaspoons vegetable oil

1 teaspoon salt

4 egg whites or 2 extralarge eggs, beaten

Apple Drizzle Topping (see page 27) or butter

FILLING

¼ cup vegetable oil

2¾ teaspoons cinnamon

Scant 1 tablespoon arrowroot or cornstarch

½ cup unsweetened apple juice concentrate (any brand)

⅓ cup chopped pecans

1. Measure flour into a large bowl and sift four times.

2. In a small bowl, stir together yeast and 2 teaspoons flour.

3. Place ½ cup concentrate and ½ cup plus 1 tablespoon water in a small saucepan and warm to 120°F. Pour over yeast mixture, stir gently to moisten, and let stand for 10 minutes.

4. In a 4-quart or larger saucepan or pot, combine 1½ cups concentrate, ½ cup plus 2 tablespoons water, oil, and salt. Heat mixture to 130°F, remove from heat, and let cool to 120°F.

5. Add 2 cups sifted flour to water-and-concentrate mixture and stir to count of 20. Add yeast mixture and stir to count of 20. Add eggs and stir to count of 20. Add 1 cup sifted flour and stir to count of 20.

6. Start timing: Knead for 10 minutes in the pan, *not on a floured surface,* gradually adding flour until the dough is soft and not sticky to the touch. Make sure you work the dough until it is smooth and elastic. Leave dough in pan, cover with a towel, and let rise in a warm place for 60 minutes. While dough is rising, make filling.

7. *To prepare filling:* In a small saucepan, stir together all filling ingredients except

nuts. Cook over medium heat, stirring constantly, until mixture thickens. *Do not boil arrowroot.* Remove pan from heat and stir well to mix in oil. Cool. Divide filling into two portions.

8. Generously coat two 13- by 9- by 2½-inch pans with vegetable shortening.

9. Using as little flour as possible (dough will be quite sticky), punch down dough, *leave in pan,* and knead for 1 minute. Let dough rest for 4 to 5 minutes, uncovered. Divide dough into two portions. Roll out each portion on a lightly floured surface to ½-inch thickness. Spread filling on dough; sprinkle with nuts. Roll up each portion of dough and filling; cut each into 1½-inch pieces (13 to 14 pieces per portion; 26 to 28 pieces total).

10. Place rolls in pans. Cover pans with towels and let rise in a warm place for 55 minutes.

11. Preheat oven to 350°F.

12. Bake about 25 minutes, or until sides and tops are slightly golden. Remove pans from oven and turn out rolls onto a large baking sheet. Using another large baking sheet, flip rolls over. Top rolls, while still warm, with Apple Drizzle Topping or butter. Serve warm or cold, or cool completely, wrap in plastic, and refrigerate or freeze. Total preparation time is approximately 3½ hours.

Yield: 26 to 28 rolls

PER ROLL (WITHOUT APPLE DRIZZLE)

Calories: 268.4	*Diabetic exchanges*
Protein: 5.2 g	*Starch:* 2
Fat: 8.1 g	*Fat:* 1½
Carbohydrate: 43.4 g	*Fruit:* 1
Sodium: 98.4 mg	

Apple Drizzle Topping

½ cup unsweetened apple juice
   concentrate (any brand)
1¾ teaspoons arrowroot or cornstarch

Generous ¼ teaspoon cinnamon
¼ cup chopped pecans

1. Place all ingredients except nuts in a small saucepan and stir well. Cook over medium heat, stirring constantly, until mixture thickens. *Do not boil arrowroot.*

2. Remove from heat and beat well. While still hot, using a large metal spoon, drizzle topping over warm rolls; sprinkle with chopped nuts.

Yield: Enough topping for one batch Apple-Nut Cinnamon Rolls (26 to 28 rolls)

PER SERVING

Calories: 17.3
Protein: 0.1 g
Fat: 0.8 g
Carbohydrate: 2.6 g

Sodium: 1.4 mg
Diabetic exchanges
  Fruit: ½

Pineapple-Orange Cinnamon Rolls

To make the preparation easier for you, I suggest having the ingredients in step 4 and in step 7 in saucepans ahead of time, ready to heat.

Knead in Pan

8½ to 9 cups all-purpose flour

2 packages yeast

2 teaspoons all-purpose flour

¼ cup plus 1 tablespoon unsweetened orange juice concentrate (Minute Maid Reduced Acid)

½ cup water

½ cup plus 3 tablespoons unsweetened apple juice concentrate (any brand)

1 cup water

½ cup plus 1 teaspoon vegetable shortening, vegetable oil, or lard

1 teaspoon salt

4 egg whites or 2 extralarge eggs, beaten

Orange Drizzle Topping for Pineapple-Orange Cinnamon Rolls (see page 30) or topping of choice (optional)

FILLING

3 tablespoons vegetable shortening, vegetable oil, or lard

2¼ teaspoons cinnamon

1 tablespoon plus ¾ teaspoon arrowroot or cornstarch

¼ cup plus 1 tablespoon plus 1½ teaspoons unsweetened apple juice concentrate (any brand)

2 tablespoons plus 1½ teaspoons unsweetened orange juice concentrate (Minute Maid Reduced Acid)

½ cup crushed, drained pineapple (drained in hand strainer)

⅓ cup chopped walnuts

1. Measure flour into a large bowl and sift four times.

2. In a small bowl, stir together yeast and 2 teaspoons flour.

3. Place ¼ cup plus 1 tablespoon orange juice concentrate and ½ cup water in a small saucepan and warm to 120°F. Pour over flour-and-yeast mixture, stir gently to moisten, and let stand for 10 minutes.

4. In a 4-quart or larger saucepan or pot, combine remaining concentrates, 1 cup water, shortening, and salt. Heat mixture to 130°F, remove from heat, and let cool to 120°F.

5. Add 2 cups sifted flour to water-and-concentrate mixture and stir to count of 20. Add yeast mixture and stir to count of 20. Add eggs and stir to count of 20. Add 1 cup sifted flour and stir to count of 20.

6. Start timing: Knead for 10 minutes in the pan, *not on a floured surface,* gradually

28

adding flour until the dough is soft and not sticky to the touch (you may not need to use all the sifted flour). Make sure you work the dough until it is smooth and elastic. Leave dough in pan, cover with a towel, and let rise in a warm place for 50 minutes. While dough is rising, make filling.

7. *To prepare filling:* In a small saucepan, stir together all filling ingredients except pineapple and nuts. Cook over medium heat, stirring constantly, until mixture thickens. *Do not boil arrowroot.* Remove pan from heat and cool. Divide filling into two portions.

8. Generously coat two 13- by 9- by 2½-inch pans with vegetable shortening.

9. Punch down dough, leave in pan, and knead for 1 minute. *Do not add flour.* Divide dough into two portions. Roll out each portion on a lightly floured surface to ½-inch thickness. Spread filling on dough and sprinkle with pineapple and nuts. Roll up each portion of dough and filling; cut each into 1½-inch pieces (13 to 14 pieces per portion; 26 to 28 pieces total).

10. Place rolls in pans. Cover pans with towels and let rise in a warm place for 45 to 50 minutes.

11. Preheat oven to 350°F.

12. Bake about 25 minutes, or until sides and tops are slightly golden. Remove pans from oven and turn out rolls onto a large baking sheet. Using another large baking sheet, flip rolls over. Top rolls, while still warm, with Orange Drizzle Topping for Pineapple-Orange Cinnamon Rolls or with topping of choice, or serve plain, either warm or cold. To store, wrap cooled rolls in plastic and refrigerate or freeze.

Yield: 26 to 28 rolls

PER ROLL (WITHOUT TOPPING)

Calories: 248.9	*Diabetic exchanges*
Protein: 5.7 g	Starch: 1½
Fat: 7 g	*Fat:* 1½
Carbohydrate: 40.6 g	*Fruit:* 1
Sodium: 94.6 mg	

Orange Drizzle Topping for Pineapple-Orange Cinnamon Rolls

2 tablespoons plus 1½ teaspoons unsweetened orange juice concentrate (Minute Maid Reduced Acid)

¼ cup plus 1 tablespoon plus 1½ teaspoons unsweetened apple juice concentrate (any brand)

1 tablespoon arrowroot or cornstarch

Generous ¼ teaspoon cinnamon

¼ cup chopped walnuts

1. Place all ingredients except nuts in a small saucepan and stir well. Cook over medium heat, stirring constantly, until mixture thickens. *Do not boil arrowroot.*

2. Remove from heat and stir well. While still hot, using a knife, drizzle topping over warm rolls; sprinkle with chopped nuts.

Yield: Enough topping for one batch of Pineapple-Orange Cinnamon Rolls (26 to 28 rolls)

PER SERVING

Calories: 17.3
Protein: 0.4 g
Fat: 0.7 g
Carbohydrate: 2.6 g

Sodium: 1 mg
Diabetic exchanges
 Fruit: ½

Marjean's Quick Sugarless Yeast Bread

Knead in Pan

6¾ cups all-purpose flour

2 packages yeast

2 teaspoons all-purpose flour

¼ cup plus 1 tablespoon unsweetened
  apple juice concentrate (any
  brand)

½ cup water

2 cups water, milk, or soy milk

¼ cup vegetable oil

2 teaspoons salt

1 to 2 tablespoons olive oil or vegetable
  oil of choice

1. Measure 6¾ cups flour into a large bowl and sift four times.

2. In a small bowl, stir together yeast and 2 teaspoons flour.

3. Place concentrate and ½ cup water in a small saucepan and warm to 120°F. Pour over flour-and-yeast mixture, stir gently to moisten, and let stand for 10 minutes.

4. In a 4-quart or larger saucepan or pot, combine 2 cups water (or milk or soy milk), ¼ cup oil, and salt. Heat mixture to 130°F, remove pan from heat, and let cool to 120°F.

5. Add 2 cups sifted flour to water-and-oil mixture and stir to count of 20. Add yeast mixture and stir to count of 20. Add 1 cup flour and stir to count of 50.

6. Start timing: Knead for 8 to 10 minutes in the pan, *not on a floured surface*, gradually adding flour until the dough is soft and not sticky to the touch (you may not need to use all the sifted flour). Make sure you work the dough until it is smooth and elastic. Leave dough in pan, cover with a towel, and let rise in a warm place for 35 to 40 minutes.

7. Oil two 9- by 5- by 2¾-inch loaf pans.

8. Place pan with dough on countertop. Uncover and let dough sit for 1 minute. *Do not punch down dough.* Dough will be sticky to the touch.

9. With a little flour on your fingers, cut dough in half with a knife and place on a *lightly* floured surface. (Use the least amount of flour you can get away with.) Gently roll out each half so that it is about 9½ by 6½ by a generous 2½ inches thick. Gently roll up each half, tucking edges under and forming a narrow loaf. Place in prepared pans. Lightly, with fingertips, cover tops of loaves with oil. Cover with a light cloth and let rise in a warm place for 35 minutes.

10. Preheat oven to 350°F.

11. Uncover loaves and bake 48 minutes, or until bread is golden brown and has a hollow sound when tapped. Remove pans from oven and turn out bread onto a wire rack. Cool for 15 minutes, brush tops with olive oil (or oil of choice), and

serve warm or cold. To store, wrap cooled loaves in plastic and store on countertop or freeze.

Yield: Two 9- by 5- by 2¾-inch loaves (24 slices)

PER SLICE

Calories: 161.6   *Sodium:* 179.6 mg
Protein: 3.9 g   *Diabetic exchanges*
Fat: 3.2 g   *Starch:* 2
Carbohydrate: 28.7 g   *Fat:* ½

WHOLE-WHEAT VARIATION: You may substitute 2 cups whole-wheat flour for 2 cups all-purpose flour in this recipe.

Tara's Sugar-Free White Bread

Knead on Floured Surface

7 cups all-purpose flour

2 packages yeast

2 teaspoons all-purpose flour

¼ cup plus 1 tablespoon unsweetened
  apple juice concentrate (any
  brand)

½ cup water

2 cups water or soy milk

Generous ¼ cup vegetable oil

2 teaspoons salt

1 to 2 tablespoons olive oil or oil of
  choice

1. Measure 7 cups flour into a large bowl and sift four times. Reserve ½ cup of sifted flour for later kneading.

2. In a small bowl, stir together yeast and 2 teaspoons flour.

3. Place concentrate and ½ cup water in a small saucepan and warm to 120°F. Pour over yeast mixture, stir gently to moisten, and let stand for 10 minutes.

4. In a 4-quart or larger saucepan or pot, combine 2 cups water (or soy milk), generous ¼ cup oil, and salt. Heat mixture to 130°F, remove pan from heat, and let cool to 120°F.

5. Add 2 cups sifted flour to water-and-oil mixture and stir to count of 20. Add yeast mixture and stir to count of 20. Add 1 cup of flour and stir to count of 20. Add rest of flour, 1 cup or less at a time, stirring flour in well before adding more.

6. Turn out dough onto a lightly floured surface and knead for 10 minutes. Gradually add more flour if needed. Make sure you work in all flour well. Dough should be soft and not sticky to the touch.

7. Oil the bottom of a large pan and place dough in pan, turning dough to coat all surfaces with oil. Cover and let rise in a warm place for 50 to 55 minutes.

8. Oil two 9- by 5- by 2¾-inch loaf pans.

9. Punch down dough and knead for 1 minute *in pan*. *Do not add flour.* Cut dough in half. On a *nonfloured* surface, gently roll out each half so that it is about 9- by 6- by 2½ inches thick. Gently turn dough over and roll very softly, maintaining the same measurements, touching it as little as possible. (This will help get rid of any bumps, etc., so bread will have a smooth top.) Gently roll up and form each half into a slender, high loaf. Tuck under edges and place in prepared pans. Lightly, with fingertips, cover tops of loaves with oil. Cover with a light cloth and let rise in a warm place for 50 to 55 minutes. After 45 minutes, preheat oven to 350°F. At this time, also check bread so you know how high it is. Dough is ready to bake when it has risen 2 inches above the sides of the pan. When the dough reaches this stage, put it in the oven and bake it as soon as possible. Remember that, since this bread uses only fruit concentrate, the yeast will run out of "food" sooner than if you were using sugar. If you allow the second rising period to go beyond the point at which the yeast runs out of food, your loaf may deflate like a popped balloon.

10. Uncover loaves and bake 50 to 55 minutes, or until bread is golden brown and has a hollow sound when tapped. Remove pans from oven and turn out bread onto a wire rack to cool. Cool for 20 to 30 minutes; brush tops with olive oil (or oil of choice). To store, wrap cooled bread in plastic and store on countertop or freeze. Total preparation time is approximately 4 hours.

Yield: Two 9- by 5- by 2¾-inch loaves (24 slices)

PER SLICE

Calories: 166.4	*Sodium:* 179.6 mg
Protein: 4.0 g	*Diabetic exchanges*
Fat: 3.2 g	*Starch:* 2
Carbohydrate: 29.7 g	*Fat:* ½

WHOLE-WHEAT VARIATION: You may substitute 2 cups whole-wheat flour and 3 heaping tablespoons wheat germ for 2 cups all-purpose flour in this recipe.

HAMBURGER-BUN VARIATION: To make hamburger buns, use two lightly oiled baking sheets and, in step 9, simply divide dough into 24 to 26 pieces and shape into buns. Follow remaining instructions, but bake for only 27 to 30 minutes, or until lightly browned. Cool on rack. Top with olive oil or oil of choice. *Yield:* 24 to 26 buns

Challah (Braided) Bread

Knead on Floured Surface

4 cups all-purpose flour
1 package yeast
1 teaspoon all-purpose flour
2 tablespoons plus 1½ teaspoons
 unsweetened apple juice
 concentrate (any brand)
⅓ cup water
⅓ cup water, milk, or soy milk

3 tablespoons plus ¾ teaspoon
 vegetable oil
¾ teaspoon salt
4 egg whites *or* 2 extralarge eggs, beaten
1 to 2 tablespoons olive oil or vegetable
 oil of choice
½ teaspoon poppy seeds

1. Measure 4 cups flour into a large bowl and sift four times. Set aside ¼ cup flour for kneading later.

2. In a small bowl, stir together yeast and 1 teaspoon flour.

3. Place concentrate and ⅓ cup water in a small saucepan and warm to 120°F. Pour over yeast mixture, stir gently to moisten, and let stand for 10 minutes.

4. In a 4-quart saucepan or pot, combine ⅓ cup water (or milk or soy milk), 3 tablespoons plus ¾ teaspoon oil, and salt. Heat mixture to 130°F, remove pan from heat, and let cool to 120°F.

5. Add ½ cup sifted flour to water-and-oil mixture and stir to count of 20. Add yeast mixture and stir to count of 20. Add eggs and stir to count of 20. Slowly add 3¼ cups sifted flour, stirring well after each addition.

6. Place dough on a lightly floured surface and knead for 10 minutes, gradually adding reserved ¼ cup sifted flour. Dough should be soft and not sticky to the touch.

7. Oil the bottom of a large pan and place dough in pan, turning dough to coat all surfaces with oil. Cover and let rise in a warm place for 50 minutes.

8. Oil or grease a large baking sheet.

9. Punch down dough, knead for 1 minute *in pan. Do not add flour. To make braid* (*do not add flour*): With a sharp knife, cut off one third of dough and set aside. Cut remaining two thirds of dough into three equal pieces. Roll each piece into a 13-inch-long rope. Place ropes side by side on prepared baking sheet. Braid the ropes beginning at the center; braid first to one end, then to the other. Pinch ends together to seal.

10. Cut remaining one third of dough into three equal pieces. Roll each piece into a 14-inch-long rope. Braid as in step 9.

11. Place small braid on top of large braid, tucking ends under. Lightly brush top of dough with olive oil (or vegetable oil of choice). Sprinkle poppy seeds over dough, pressing lightly to keep seeds in place. Cover with a light cloth and let rise in a warm place for 50 minutes. After 45 minutes, preheat oven to 350°F. At this time, check bread so you know how high it is. Dough is ready to bake when it has doubled in bulk. When the dough reaches this stage, put it in the oven and bake it as soon as possible. Remember that, since this bread uses only fruit concentrate, the yeast will run out of "food" sooner than if you were using sugar. If you allow the second rising period to go beyond the point at which the yeast runs out of food, your loaf may deflate like a popped balloon.

12. Uncover loaf and bake 37 to 39 minutes, or until golden brown. Remove baking sheet from oven and turn out bread onto a wire rack. Cool for 15 minutes before serving. Serve warm or cool completely before wrapping in plastic and storing on countertop or freezer.

Yield: One 13- by 5- by 3½-inch loaf (14 slices)

PER SLICE

Calories: 179.2	*Sodium:* 131.6 mg
Protein: 4.9 g	*Diabetic exchanges*
Fat: 4.6 g	Starch: 2
Carbohydrate: 29.0 g	Fat: 1

Holiday Fig- or Date-Cinnamon Ring

Knead on Floured Surface
No Egg

6¼ cups all-purpose flour

2 packages yeast

2 teaspoons all-purpose flour

¼ cup plus 1 tablespoon unsweetened apple juice concentrate (any brand)

½ cup water

1¼ cups water

Generous ⅓ cup vegetable oil

¾ teaspoon salt

1 tablespoon olive oil or vegetable oil of choice

FILLING

1¼ cups packed, chopped (cut with scissors) Calimyrna figs, or dried Black Mission figs, or a combination of both; or dates (if using dates, you will need 32 of them)

½ cup water

1½ teaspoons cinnamon

¾ cup chopped pecans

Generous 1 tablespoon water

1. Measure 6¼ cups flour into a large bowl and sift four times. Reserve ¼ cup of sifted flour for later kneading.

2. In a small bowl, stir together yeast and 2 teaspoons flour.

3. Place concentrate and ½ cup water in a small saucepan and warm to 120°F. Pour over yeast mixture, stir gently to moisten, and let stand for 10 minutes.

4. In a 4-quart or larger saucepan or pot, combine 1¼ cups water, generous ⅓ cup oil, and salt. Heat mixture to 130°F, remove pan from heat, and let cool to 120°F.

5. Add a generous 1½ cups sifted flour to water-and-oil mixture and stir to count of 20. Add yeast mixture and stir to count of 20. Add 1 cup flour and stir to count of 20. Add remaining flour, 1 cup or less at a time, stirring flour in well before adding more.

6. Place dough onto a lightly floured surface and knead for 8 minutes. Add more flour if necessary, until dough is soft and not sticky to the touch.

7. Oil the bottom of a large pan and place dough in pan, turning dough to coat all surfaces with oil. Cover and let rise in a warm place until doubled in bulk—45 to 50 minutes. While dough is rising, make filling.

8. *To prepare filling:* In a small saucepan, stir together figs or dates and ½ cup water. Bring mixture to a boil over medium heat, stirring constantly, and simmer

until thick (about 5 minutes). Remove pan from heat. Stir in cinnamon and pecans and 1 generous tablespoon water. Stir well; set aside to cool.

9. Generously oil or grease a 10- by 4-inch tube pan.

10. Punch down dough, knead for 1 minute *in pan. Do not* add flour while kneading. Place dough on a lightly floured surface. Roll out dough to form a rectangle approximately 15 by 18 inches. Stir filling mixture well and spread evenly over rolled-out dough, leaving a ½-inch border of dough along the long edges.

11. Roll up dough jelly-roll style. Pinch long seam together; join ends and pinch them together to form a ring.

12. Place ring into prepared pan and gently coat dough with oil, using your fingertips. Cover pan with a towel and let rise in a warm place for 35 to 40 minutes.

13. Preheat oven to 350°F.

14. Using scissors, make six V-shaped cuts, each ½ inch deep by 2 inches long by 1 inch wide at the wide end of the V. The narrow end of each V should point outward. Cover pan and wait for oven to reach baking temperature—approximately 5 minutes.

15. Bake for 35 minutes, cover top with aluminum foil (so it won't burn), and continue baking for another 20 to 21 minutes, or until top and sides of ring are lightly golden.

16. Remove pan from oven and carefully turn out ring onto wire rack. Turn ring right side up. Cool for 30 minutes and cover with olive oil (or oil of choice). Serve warm, plain, or with topping of choice. This bread makes excellent toast in the morning or can be served cold to dress up any meal. To store, wrap cooled ring in plastic and refrigerate, freeze, or store on countertop.

Yield: One 10- by 5½-inch tube loaf (18 slices)

PER SLICE

Calories: 289.3	*Diabetic exchanges*
Protein: 5.7 g	*Starch:* 2
Fat: 8.7 g	*Fat:* 1½
Carbohydrate: 47.0 g	*Fruit:* 1
Sodium: 93.3 mg	

Banana or Pear Yeast Bread

No Concentrate
Knead on Floured Surface

2 bananas or 2 pears, peeled, cored, and sliced	½ cup water
½ cup water (for cooking)	1½ cups water
7 cups all-purpose flour	Generous ¼ cup vegetable oil
2 packages yeast	1½ teaspoons salt
1 tablespoon all-purpose flour	1 to 2 tablespoons olive oil or oil of choice

1. In a small saucepan, combine bananas (or pears) and ½ cup water and bring to a slow boil over medium heat. Cook bananas for ½ hour (pears for 1 hour), adding a little water as needed while fruit is cooking so fruit does not burn. When finished cooking, remove pan from heat, mash fruit, and cool. You will need ¾ cup cooked fruit to use in place of fruit concentrate. When cooked fruit is cool, measure out ¾ cup. Add more water if needed to make ¾ cup of fruit mixture.

2. Measure 7 cups flour into a large bowl and sift four times. Reserve ½ cup of sifted flour for later kneading.

3. In a small bowl, stir together yeast and 1 tablespoon flour.

4. Place ½ cup water and ¼ cup of fruit mixture in a small saucepan and warm to 120°F. Pour over yeast mixture, stir gently to moisten, and let stand for 10 minutes.

5. In a 4-quart or larger saucepan or pot, combine 1½ cups water, ½ cup fruit mixture, salt, and oil. Heat mixture to 130°F. Remove pan from heat and let cool to 120°F.

6. Add 2 cups sifted flour to water-and-oil mixture and stir to count of 20. Add yeast mixture and stir to count of 20. Add 1 cup of flour and stir to count of 20. Add rest of flour, 1 cup or less at a time, stirring flour in well before adding more.

7. Turn out dough onto a lightly floured surface and knead for 10 minutes. Gradually add more flour if needed. Make sure you work in all flour well. Dough should be soft and not sticky to the touch.

8. Oil the bottom of a large pan and place dough in pan, turning dough to coat all surfaces with oil. Cover and let rise in a warm place for 50 to 55 minutes.

9. Oil two 9- by 5- by 2¾-inch loaf pans.

10. Punch down dough and knead for 1 minute *in pan. Do not add flour.* Cut dough in half. On a *nonfloured* surface, gently roll out each half so that it is about 9 by 6 by 2½ inches thick. Gently turn dough over and roll very softly, maintaining the same measurements, touching it as little as possible. (This will help get rid of any bumps, etc., so bread will have a smooth top.) Gently roll up and form each half into a slender, high loaf. Tuck under edges and place in prepared pans. Lightly, with fingertips, cover tops of loaves with oil. Cover with a light cloth and let rise in a warm place for 50 to 55 minutes. (Check bread after 45 minutes so you know how high it is.) Dough is ready to bake when it has risen 2 inches above the sides of the pan. When the dough reaches this stage, put it in the oven and bake it as soon as possible. Remember that, since this bread uses only fruit, the yeast will run out of "food" sooner than if you were using sugar. If you allow the second rising period to go beyond the point at which the yeast runs out of food, your loaf may deflate like a popped balloon.

11. Preheat oven to 350°F.

12. Uncover loaves and bake 50 to 55 minutes, or until bread is golden brown and has a hollow sound when tapped. Remove pans from oven and turn out bread onto a wire rack to cool. Cool for 20 to 30 minutes and brush tops with olive oil (or oil of choice). Store cooled loaves in plastic on countertop or freeze.

Yield: Two 9- by 5- by 2¾-inch loaves (24 slices)

PER SLICE

Calories: 159
Protein: 3.9 g
Fat: 3.1 g
Carbohydate: 28.4 g
Sodium: 123.0 mg

Diabetic exchanges
   Starch: 1
   Fat: ½
   Fruit: 1

Spelt Whole-Grain Yeast Bread

Has Gluten

Knead on Floured Surface

7¼ cups spelt whole-grain flour

2 packages yeast

2 teaspoons spelt whole-grain flour

¼ cup plus 1 tablespoon unsweetened apple juice concentrate (any brand)

½ cup water

2 cups water

Generous ¼ cup vegetable oil

Scant 2 teaspoons salt

1 to 2 tablespoons olive oil or oil of choice

1. Measure out 7¼ cups of spelt whole-grain flour into a large bowl and sift four times. Reserve ½ cup of sifted flour for later kneading.

2. In a small bowl, stir together yeast and 2 teaspoons spelt whole-grain flour.

3. Place concentrate and ½ cup water in a small saucepan and warm to 120°F. Pour over yeast mixture, stir gently to moisten, and let stand for 10 minutes.

4. In a 4-quart or larger saucepan or pot, combine 2 cups water, generous ¼ cup oil, and salt. Heat mixture to 125°F, remove pan from heat, and let cool to 120°F.

5. Add 2 cups sifted spelt whole-grain flour to water-and-oil mixture and stir to count of 20. Add yeast mixture and stir to count of 20. Add 1½ cups of sifted flour and stir to count of 20. Add rest of flour, 1 cup or less at a time, stirring flour in well before adding more.

6. Turn out dough onto a lightly floured surface (use spelt whole-grain flour) and knead for 9 minutes. Gradually add more flour if needed. Make sure you work in all flour well. Dough should be soft and not sticky to the touch.

7. Oil the bottom of a large pan and place dough in pan. Turn dough to coat all surfaces with oil. Cover and let rise in a warm place for 40 to 43 minutes.

8. Oil two 9- by 5- by 2¾-inch loaf pans.

9. Punch down dough and knead for 1 minute *in pan. Do not add flour.* Cut dough in half. On a *nonfloured* surface, gently roll out each half so that it is about 9 by 6 by 2 inches thick. Gently turn dough over and roll very softly, maintaining the same measurements, touching it as little as possible. (This will get rid of any bumps, etc., so bread will have a smooth top.) Gently roll up and form each half into a slender, high loaf. Tuck under edges and place in prepared pans. Lightly, with fingertips,

cover tops of loaves with oil. Cover with a light cloth and let rise in a warm place for 40 to 45 minutes.

10. After 30 minutes, preheat oven to 350°F. At this time, also check bread so you know how high it is. Dough is ready to bake when it has risen 2 inches above the sides of the pan. When the dough reaches this stage, put it in the oven and bake it as soon as possible. Remember that, since this bread uses only fruit concentrate, the yeast will run out of "food" sooner than if you were using sugar. If you allow the second rising period to go beyond the point at which the yeast runs out of food, your loaf may deflate like a popped balloon.

11. Uncover loaves and bake 50 to 53 minutes, or until bread is golden brown and has a hollow sound when tapped. Remove pans from oven and turn out bread onto a wire rack to cool. Cool for about 20 to 30 minutes; brush tops with olive oil (or oil of choice). To store, wrap cooled bread in plastic and place on countertop or freeze. Total preparation time is approximately 4 hours.

Yield: Two 9- by 5- 2¾-inch loaves (24 slices)

PER SLICE

Calories: 166.5
Protein: 6.3 g
Fat: 4.1 g
Carbohydrate: 29.7 g
Sodium: 178.9 mg

Diabetic exchanges
　Starch: 1
　Fat: 1
　Fruit: 1

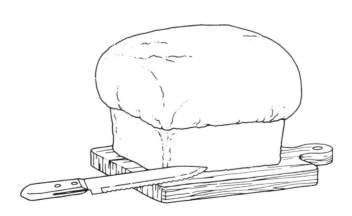

Pizza

CRUST

1 package yeast	½ teaspoon salt
3 tablespoons water	1½ cups all-purpose flour
1 tablespoon unsweetened apple juice concentrate (any brand)	
¼ cup water, milk, or soy milk	Pizza toppings of your choice (tomato sauce, sausage, peppers, onion,
¼ cup vegetable shortening or lard	cheese, mushrooms, etc.)

1. Place yeast in a small bowl.
2. Place 3 tablespoons water and concentrate in a small saucepan and warm to 120°F. Pour water and concentrate over yeast and let stand for 10 minutes.
3. In a large saucepan, combine ¼ cup water (or milk or soy milk), shortening, and salt. Heat mixture to 130°F, remove pan from heat, and let cool to 120°F.
4. Add ⅓ cup flour to water mixture and stir. Add yeast and stir. Add remaining flour to make a soft dough.
5. Place dough on a lightly floured surface and knead for 5 minutes. Place dough in a lightly oiled bowl, turn, cover with a towel, and let rise in a warm place for 1 hour.
6. Preheat oven to 425°F.
7. Turn dough onto an oiled or greased 12-inch pizza pan, spread out evenly using your fingers, and add desired toppings.
8. Bake 10 minutes; reduce oven temperature to 400°F and bake 8 minutes more, or until bottom of pizza crust is streaked with gold. Remove pan from oven. Serve hot.

Yield: One 12-inch pizza (8 slices)

PER SLICE (WITHOUT TOPPINGS; CRUST ONLY)

Calories: 148.2	*Sodium:* 134.7 mg
Protein: 2.8 g	*Diabetic exchanges*
Fat: 6.7 g	*Starch:* 1½
Carbohydrate: 19.1 g	*Fat:* 1

Potato Pizza Crust

Gluten-Free
Contains Egg Yolks; not Cholesterol-Free

CRUST:

¼ cup potato flour

2 extralarge eggs

½ cup Ener-G Brand Potato Mix (contains corn-free baking powder); fill ½ cup generously, press down with side of knife, level off

3 tablespoons plus 1 teaspoon potato flour; measure as with Potato Mix

Generous ½ teaspoon salt

2¾ teaspoons Featherweight baking powder (cereal-free) or homemade baking powder

1½ teaspoons unsweetened apple juice concentrate (any brand)

2 tablespoons vegetable oil

¼ cup water

pizza toppings of your choice: tomato sauce, diced vegetables (fresh, pre-boiled or stir-fried, drained well), browned and drained meats, spices, diced onion, sliced mushrooms, sliced olives, etc.

1. Prepare pizza toppings. Keep warm.

2. Preheat oven to 350°F. Oil a 12-inch pizza pan. Place ¼ cup potato flour in a small bowl to be used later for patting out the dough.

3. Separate eggs, placing the yolks in a large-sized bowl and the egg whites in a small-sized bowl. Using a hand-operated mechanical beater, beat egg whites until very stiff. They should not fall out when the bowl is turned upside down. Set whites aside.

4. In a small-sized bowl and using a spoon, stir together potato mix, potato flour, salt, and baking powder. Mix well. Set aside.

5. Add concentrate, oil, and water to egg yolks. Whip, using a hand-operated mechanical beater to mix ingredients well. Rebeat egg whites to make sure they are stiff.

6. Pour potato mixture into egg yolk-and-concentrate mixture. Combine ingredients well. Quickly fold stiff egg whites into batter, distributing the whites well.

7. Pour dough onto prepared pizza pan. The dough is quite sticky! Using potato flour on the bottoms of your hands, pat out the dough *very lightly* over the pan's surface. The air in the egg whites is needed to ensure that the crust gets done. You can make an 8-inch thick-crust pizza or a 12-inch thin-crust pizza. Add more flour to hands as needed.

8. Bake 15 minutes. The top of the crust should be lightly golden in spots, the bottom should be lightly browned all over. Remove pan from oven. Turn oven down to 300°F. Add desired pizza toppings to pizza crust and place pizza back in oven to bake for 5 minutes or so to warm everything through. Remove pan from oven. Serve hot.

Yield: One 8-inch thich-crust pizza or one 12-inch thin-crust pizza (8 slices)

PER SLICE (WITHOUT TOPPINGS; CRUST ONLY)

Calories: 124.9   *Sodium:* 158.7 mg
Protein: 2.8 g   *Diabetic exchanges*
Fat: 4.9 g   *Starch:* 1
Carbohydrate: 17.6 g   *Fat: 1*

CAKES
AND
CUPCAKES

For most people, cakes are an important symbol. They evoke memories of Grandma's kitchen—of mixing bowls and batter-covered spoons. They are an essential part of every birthday and important celebration. And they are the essence of baking—the one item that every cook wants to get "just right" and the item they take most pride in serving.

Most cakes, however, call for refined sugar, so it is with great pride that I present these next recipes, all made only with natural fruit sweeteners. I hope they will bring back the sense of celebration to those who may have thought they could no longer eat cake.

These cakes do not really need toppings; they are great just the way they are! Each cake has a distinct taste and flavor of its own. I've always believed that the cake itself is the important thing; however, I realize that you may want to dress up these cakes—and that's fine. Use your imagination and the following hints as your guide.

FROSTING AND ICING HINTS FOR CAKES

Try any of the following as frostings and toppings:

- Flavored Coconut Spreads for Cakes (see page 51). These can be used on any cake and there are many different flavors to choose from. The choice is up to you. Sprinkle Flavored Coconut Spreads with chopped nuts, if desired;
- any commercial whipped topping (please read labels carefully because some contain sugar, corn syrup, caseinate or whey, milk products, or Equal, which contains corn), sprinkled with chopped nuts, moistened coconut, or sliced fruit, if desired;

- sliced fresh fruit such as strawberries, kiwis, ripe peaches, bananas, or dark cherries;
- pureed fresh fruit such as blueberries or raspberries;
- any all-fruit jam or jelly (this could be thinned with a little water or fruit juice and heated to make a glaze that is easy to spread over cooled cake);
- whipped cream cheese, with or without nuts (especially good on Orange-Carrot Cake, page 71);
- plain yogurt, topped with sliced fresh fruit or chopped nuts, if desired.

LAYER CAKES

The following cakes can be turned into layer cakes simply by switching from one type of baking pan to another. (For information on turning the cake batter into layers, see the instructions at the end of each recipe. Apply the frosting of your choice between layers and on top.)

- Chocolate-Date Cake (page 54)
- Milk Chocolate Cake (page 58)
- Golden Harvest Cake (page 70)
- Orange-Carrot Cake (page 71)
- Apple-Orange Poppy Seed Cake (page 73)
- Pineapple-Cherry Upside-Down Cake (batter only; page 79)
- Walnut-Raisin Cake (page 64)
- Spice Cake (page 67)
- Apple-Potato Layer Cake (page 74)

CUPCAKES

Cupcakes are a special treat for kids and make wonderful lunchbox desserts. These five cake recipes will make excellent cupcakes:

- Chocolate-Date Cake (page 54)

- Golden Harvest Cake (page 70)
- Orange-Carrot Cake (page 71)
- Apple-Orange Poppy Seed Cake (page 73)
- Pineapple-Cherry Upside-Down Cake (batter only; page 79)
- Walnut-Raisin Cake (page 64)
- Spice Cake (page 67)

For information on turning the cake batter into cupcakes, see the instructions at the end of each recipe.

Make sure you have supplies ready before starting recipes.

SUBSTITUTIONS

Remember that 1 whole egg is interchangeable with every 2 egg whites used in these cake recipes.

Carob powder and cocoa powder are also interchangeable in these recipes, but you should be aware that most brands of carob contain milk and most brands of cocoa contain cornstarch. Read labels and call the companies if you are in doubt and have allergies. For milk-free recipes, use cocoa; for corn-free recipes, use carob. For milk-free, corn-free recipes, use chocolate. For each 3 tablespoons of carob or cocoa powder, use 1 square of chocolate and decrease the milk, water, or other liquid in the recipe by 1 tablespoon. (*Note:* A spokesperson for the Hershey Chocolate Company has stated that Hershey adds neither corn nor dairy products to its cocoa. A spokesperson for General Foods Corporation has stated that the company adds neither corn nor dairy products to its Baker's All-Natural Unsweetened Chocolate.)

Finally, remember to read each recipe thoroughly in advance. You will want to make sure all the ingredients are ready before you start.

Flavored Coconut Spread for Cake

For a 9-inch by 9-inch cake

Try Flavored Coconut Spread on any cake. The flavorings I suggest are pleasantly sweet and mild, but if you find you want a little more fruit flavor, increase the amount of unsweetened concentrate a little. You can also use Basic Recipe as is, without flavoring. (See *note*) Cool spread for 3½ to 4 hours before use.

BASIC RECIPE

½ cup *dry* unsweetened fine coconut

1½ cups water

1 tablespoon plus 1 teaspoon vegetable oil

2 tablespoons Minute Tapioca

Suggested flavorings: (choose 1)

½ teaspoon pure vanilla

2 tablespoons unsweetened black cherry juice concentrate (K. W. Knudsen Family or Tree of Life)

2 tablespoons unsweetened white grape juice concentrate (Welch's)

2 tablespoons unsweetened apple juice concentrate (any brand) plus ½ teaspoon cinnamon

2 tablespoons unsweetened apple juice concentrate (any brand)

1 tablespoon unsweetened orange juice concentrate (Minute Maid Reduced Acid) plus 1 tablespoon unsweetened apple juice concetrate (any brand)

Optional: Chopped nuts to sprinkle on cake

1. In a medium-sized saucepan, stir together all ingredients except the nuts. Allow mixture to sit for 5 minutes.

2. Place saucepan over medium heat and bring mixture to a boil, stirring constantly. Continue boiling and stirring for 1 minute, then remove pan from heat and allow mixture to cool.

3. When mixture has cooled for 3½ to 4 hours, stir, and then spread over cooled cake. Sprinkle with chopped nuts, if you wish.

Yield: 1½ cups Coconut Spread, enough for one 9-inch by 9-inch cake (9 servings)

PER SERVING (WITHOUT FLAVORING)

Calories: 55.3

Protein: 0.3 g

Fat: 4.8 g

Carbohydrate: 3.3g

Sodium: 1.6 mg

Diabetic exchanges

  Fat: 1

Note: If you are going to freeze your cake, *do not* frost with Coconut Spread. Coconut Spread does not freeze well and separates when frozen. Use Coconut Spread only when fresh. It stays good for 3 days.

Flavored Coconut Spread for Cake

For a 9-inch by 13-inch cake or two 9-inch square cakes

Cool spread for 3½ to 4 hours before use (see *Note*).

BASIC RECIPE

¾ cup *dry* unsweetened fine coconut
2¼ cups water
2 tablespoons vegetable oil
3 tablespoons Minute Tapioca
Suggested flavorings: (choose 1)
¾ teaspoon pure vanilla
3 tablespoons unsweetened black cherry juice concentrate (K. W. Knudsen Family or Tree of Life
3 tablespoons unsweetened white grape juice concentrate (Welch's)
3 tablespoons unsweetened apple juice concentrate (any brand) plus ¾ teaspoon cinnamon
3 tablespoons unsweetened apple juice concentrate (any brand)
1 tablespoon plus 1½ teaspoon unsweetened orange juice concentrate (Minute Maid Reduced Acid) plus 1 tablespoon plus 1½ teaspoon unsweetened apple juice concentrate (any brand)
Optional: chopped nuts to sprinkle on cake

1. In a large-sized saucepan, stir together all ingredients except the nuts. Allow mixture to sit for 5 minutes.

2. Place saucepan over medium heat and bring mixture to a boil, stirring constantly. Continue boiling and stirring for 1 minute, then remove pan from heat and allow mixture to cool.

3. When mixture has cooled for 3½ to 4 hours, stir, and then spread over cooled cake. Sprinkle with chopped nuts, if you wish.

Yield: 2¼ cups Coconut Spread, enough for one 9-inch by 13-inch cake (15 servings)

PER SERVING (WITHOUT FLAVORING)

Calories: 49.8 *Sodium:* 1.4 mg
Protein: 0.3 g *Diabetic exchanges*
Fat: 4.3 g *Fat:* 1
Carbohydrate: 3.0 g

Note: If you are going to freeze your cake, *do not* frost with Coconut Spread. Coconut Spread does not freeze well and separates when frozen. Use Coconut Spread only when fresh. It stays good for 3 days.

Chocolate-Date Cake

No Eggs

1¾ cups all-purpose flour, tapped lightly 4 to 5 times

1 cup packed date sugar

¼ cup plus 1 tablespoon unsweetened cocoa powder or unsweetened carob powder (see page 000)

½ teaspoon salt

⅓ cup vegetable oil

¼ cup unsweetened purple grape juice concentrate (any brand)

¼ cup unsweetened apple juice concentrate (any brand)

1 cup plus 3 tablespoons plus 2 teaspoons water

1½ teaspoons baking soda

Chocolate-Date Frosting (see page 55)

1. Preheat oven to 325°F. Oil a 9- by 9- by 2-inch baking pan.

2. In a large bowl, using a fork, stir together flour, date sugar, cocoa, and salt. Set aside.

3. In a medium-sized bowl, combine oil, concentrates, and water. Beat mixture for 30 seconds with a hand-operated mechanical beater. Add concentrate mixture to flour mixture and beat well, by hand, for 4 minutes. Stir in baking soda quickly, and then mix (28 to 30 beats); immediately pour mixture into prepared baking pan.

4. Bake 40 minutes, or until a cake tester inserted in center of cake comes out clean.

5. Remove pan from oven and place on a wire rack until cake is completely cooled. Frost with Chocolate-Date Frosting. To store, place frosted cake in airtight container and store on countertop or freeze.

Yield: One 9- by 9- by 2-inch cake (9 servings)

PER SERVING (WITHOUT ICING)

Calories: 250.8

Protein: 3.1 g

Fat: 8.8 g

Carbohydrate: 41.3 g

Sodium: 331.3 mg

Diabetic exchanges

Starch: 1

Fat: 1½

Fruit: 1½

CUPCAKE VARIATION: This Chocolate-Date Cake is very moist and therefore makes excellent cupcakes. Follow the same instructions as for the cake, but use 16 or 17 muffin cups (with paper liners) and reduce the baking time to 17 to 19 minutes (at 325°F). Use a cake tester to test for doneness. When done, remove tins from oven and remove cupcakes to a table or wire rack to cool. Frost with Chocolate-Date Frosting.

LAYER-CAKE VARIATIONS: For an 8½-inch round layer cake, simply pour batter into two generously oiled or greased (or grease bottom and sides of pans and place waxed paper on pan bottoms) 8½-inch round cake pans. Bake 24 to 26 minutes at 325°F. Use a cake tester to test for doneness. Remove pans from oven and place on a wire rack. Cool 10 minutes before loosening cake from sides of pan with a knife and removing cake from pan. To frost the center, top, and sides of cake, double the recipe for Chocolate-Date Frosting.

For a 9-inch round layer cake, simply pour batter into two generously oiled or greased (or grease bottom and sides of pans and place waxed paper on pan bottoms) 9-inch round cake pans. Bake 22 to 24 minutes at 325°F. Use a cake tester to test for doneness. Follow rest of instructions given in preceding 8½-inch Layer-Cake Variation.

Chocolate-Date Frosting

1 ounce (1 square) Baker's All-Natural Unsweetened Chocolate
1 tablespoon vegetable oil
5 tablespoons water
½ cup date sugar

1. In a small saucepan, melt chocolate, oil, and water over medium heat.
2. Reduce heat to low, add date sugar, and cook, stirring, for 2 to 2½ minutes.
3. Remove pan from heat and continue to stir mixture for 1 to 2 minutes. Spread frosting on cooled cake.

Yield: Enough frosting for one 9- by 9- by 2-inch cake, or 16 or 17 cupcakes (9 servings). Double recipe to frost center, top, and sides of a layer cake.

PER SERVING

Calories: 51
Protein: 0.6 g
Fat: 3.1 g
Carbohydrate: 6.2 g
Sodium: 0.1 mg
Diabetic exchanges
  Fat: ⅔
  Fruit: ⅓

Nutty No-Sugar Brownies

½ cup plus 3 tablespoons vegetable oil
1½ cups date sugar, tapped well
½ cup minus 1½ teaspoons water
6 egg whites *or* 3 extralarge eggs
¾ cup all-purpose flour
½ cup well-packed unsweetened cocoa
   powder or unsweetened carob
   powder (see page 50)

½ teaspoon salt
½ cup chopped nuts
¾ teaspoon baking soda

1. Preheat oven to 350°F. Oil the bottom only of a 9- by 9- by 2-inch baking pan.

2. In a large bowl, stir together all ingredients except baking soda until well combined. Stir in baking soda quickly, and then mix (28 to 30 beats); immediately pour mixture into prepared baking pan.

3. Bake 20 minutes at 350°F. Turn down oven to 325°F and bake another 15 minutes, or until a cake tester inserted in center of brownies comes out clean.

4. Remove pan from oven and place on a wire rack. Cool 30 minutes before cutting brownies, with a knife, into squares for serving. To store, place cooled brownies in an airtight container and store on countertop or freeze.

Yield: 9 servings

PER SERVING (USING WALNUTS FOR CHOPPED NUTS)

Calories: 315
Protein: 6.3 g
Fat: 21.7 g
Carbohydrate: 27.0 g

Sodium: 70.3 mg
Diabetic exchanges
   Starch: 1¾
   Fat: 4¼

Chocolate-Coconut Cake

½ cup unsweetened fine coconut, premoistened with 2 teaspoons water and 2 teaspoons vegetable oil

4 egg whites or 2 extralarge eggs

⅓ cup plus ½ teaspoon vegetable oil

¼ cup unsweetened white grape juice concentrate (Welch's)

¼ cup plus 2 tablespoons unsweetened apple juice concentrate (any brand)

⅓ cup unsweetened black cherry juice concentrate (K. W. Knudsen Family or Tree of Life)

½ teaspoon cherry flavor (see *Note*)

1¼ cups all-purpose flour

¼ cup plus 1 tablespoon firmly packed unsweetened cocoa powder or unsweetened carob powder (see page 50)

1 teaspoon baking soda

2¼ teaspoons baking powder

Topping: 4 tablespoons unsweetened fine coconut, premoistened with 1 teaspoon vegetable oil and 1 teaspoon water, 2 tablespoons chopped pecans

1. Preheat oven to 325°F. Oil and flour a 9- by 9- by 2-inch baking pan. Measure out ½ cup unsweetened fine coconut and premoisten with water and oil; stir and set aside.

2. In a large bowl, combine eggs, oil, concentrates, and cherry flavor. Beat mixture for 30 seconds with a hand-operated mechanical beater. Add flour, cocoa, and coconut and beat well. Stir in baking soda and baking powder quickly, and then mix (28 to 30 beats); immediately pour mixture into prepared baking pan.

3. Bake 28 to 29 minutes, or until a cake tester inserted in center of cake comes out clean. This cake settles slightly.

4. Remove pan from oven and place on a wire rack until cake is completely cooled. While cake is cooling, combine topping ingredients. Stir well and let coconut absorb moisture. Sprinkle over cooled cake. To store, cover cooled cake in plastic and store on countertop or freeze.

Yield: One 9- by 9- by 2-inch cake (9 servings)

PER SERVING

Calories: 286.2	*Diabetic exchanges*
Protein: 4.6 g	*Starch:* 1
Fat: 15.8 g	*Fat:* 3
Carbohydrate: 31.8 g	*Fruit:* 1
Sodium: 296.9 mg	

Note: You can purchase natural (alcohol-free) cherry flavor at health-food stores. I've used the Frontier brand. Cherry flavor contains glycerin, natural flavors, and water.

Milk Chocolate Cake

2 cups frozen, dark, sweet cherries, partially thawed
2 to 4 tablespoons water
4 egg whites *or* 2 extralarge eggs
⅓ cup vegetable oil
¼ cup unsweetened purple or white grape juice concentrate (any brand)
¼ cup unsweetened apple juice concentrate (any brand)

1 tablespoon plus 2 teaspoons soy powder *or* 4 tablespoons dry milk powder *or* 1 tablespoon plus 2 teaspoons all-purpose flour
1⅓ cups all-purpose flour, tapped lightly 4 to 5 times
¼ cup firmly packed unsweetened cocoa powder or unsweetened carob powder (see page 50)
1¼ teaspoons baking soda

1. Preheat oven to 325°F. Oil and flour a 9- by 9- by 2-inch baking pan.

2. Puree partially thawed frozen cherries and water in a blender. Blend until mixture turns and folds. Place puree in a small strainer over a small bowl and let drain for 10 minutes, stirring occasionally. Pour pulp remaining in strainer into a measuring cup and add enough of the juice to make ¾ cup of pulp and juice.

3. In a large bowl, combine ¾ cup cherry pulp and juice, eggs, oil, concentrates, and soy powder (or dry milk or flour). Beat mixture for 30 seconds with a hand-operated mechanical beater. Add 1⅓ cups flour and cocoa; beat well. Stir in baking soda quickly, and then mix (28 to 30 beats); immediately pour mixture into prepared baking pan.

4. Bake 30 to 31 minutes, or until a cake tester inserted in center of cake comes out clean.

5. Remove pan from oven and place on a wire rack until cake is completely cooled. To store, cover cooled cake with plastic wrap or in an airtight container and store on countertop or freeze.

Yield: One 9- by 9- by 2-inch cake (9 servings)

PER SERVING

Calories: 211.4   *Diabetic exchanges*
Protein: 4.5 g   *Starch:* 1
Fat: 8.7 g   *Fat:* 1½
Carbohydrate: 29.4 g   *Fruit:* 1
Sodium: 202 mg

MILK CHOCOLATE LAYER-CAKE VARIATIONS: For an 8½-inch round layer cake, simply pour batter into two generously oiled or greased and floured (or grease bottom and sides of pans and place waxed paper on pan bottoms) 8½-inch round cake pans. Bake at 325°F for 21 to 23 minutes, or until a cake tester inserted in center of cake comes out clean. Remove pans from oven and place on a wire rack. Cool 10 minutes before loosening cake from sides of pans with a knife and removing cakes from pans. Apply frosting of your choice between layers and on top.

For an 8½-inch round four-layer cake, just double the batter and use four 8½-inch round layer cake pans.

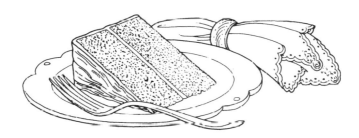

Cherry-Carob Potato Cake

Gluten-Free

2 cups frozen, dark, sweet cherries (slightly thawed to thawed)

¼ cup water

4 egg whites or 2 extralarge eggs

Generous ⅓ cup vegetable oil

½ cup unsweetened black cherry concentrate (Tree of Life or R. W. Knudsen Family)

1 cup minus 1 tablespoon Ener-G Brand Potato Mix

¼ cup packed unsweetened carob powder

1½ teaspoons baking soda

1. Preheat oven to 325°F. Oil an 8- by 8- by 2-inch glass baking dish.

2. Puree cherries and water in a blender. Blend on high, until mixture turns and folds. Place puree in a small strainer over a small bowl and let drain for 10 minutes, stirring occasionally. Pour pulp remaining in strainer into a measuring cup and add enough of the juice to make ¾ cup of pulp and juice.

3. In a large bowl, combine ¾ cup cherry pulp and juice, eggs, oil, and concentrate. Beat mixture for 30 to 40 seconds with a hand-operated mechanical beater, until foamy. Add potato mix and carob powder; beat well. Stir in baking soda quickly, and then mix (28 to 30 beats); immediately pour mixture into prepared baking dish.

4. Bake about 33 to 34 minutes, or until a cake tester inserted in center of cake comes out clean.

5. Remove dish from oven and place on a wire rack until cake is completely cooled. To store, cover cooled cake well with plastic wrap or in an airtight container and store on countertop or freeze. This cake tends to dry out quickly. The middle of the cake settles slightly and forms a ridge around outside border of cake. This is normal.

Yield: One 8- by 8- by 2-inch cake (9 servings)

PER SERVING

Calories: 216.7

Protein: 2.2 g

Fat: 8.1 g

Carbohydrate: 30.4 g

Sodium: 284 mg

Diabetic exchanges

Starch: 1

Fat: 1½

Fruit: 1

Pineapple-Apple Cake

TOPPING

1 cup unsweetened flaked or fine coconut, premoistened with 1 tablespoon plus 1 teaspoon vegetable oil and 1 tablespoon plus 1 teaspoon water

½ cup unsweetened diced pineapple chunks, drained

¾ cup peeled, cored, and diced apple

½ teaspoon cinnamon

¼ cup chopped walnuts

CAKE

Generous ½ cup unsweetened diced pineapple chunks, drained

6 egg whites or 3 extralarge eggs

⅓ cup plus 1 teaspoon vegetable oil

1½ cups unsweetened apple juice concentrate (any brand)

Generous 3 teaspoons cinnamon

2 cups plus 2 tablespoons all-purpose flour

2½ teaspoons baking soda

1. Preheat oven to 325°F. Grease and flour a 13- by 9- by 2-inch baking pan.

2. *To make topping:* In a medium-sized bowl, place coconut and premoisten. Stir and set aside. Dice pineapple and measure out ½ cup. Place diced pineapple in hand strainer over a small bowl and press lightly with a spoon to reduce moisture content. Set aside to drain. Combine apple and coconut. Add cinnamon and chopped nuts. Stir in drained pineapple, mixing well. Set aside.

3. *To make batter:* Dice pineapple and measure out a generous ½ cup. Place pineapple in a hand strainer and press lightly with a spoon to reduce moisture content. Set aside to drain.

4. In a large bowl, combine eggs, oil, and concentrate. Beat for 1 minute using a hand-operated mechanical beater. Add pineapple and stir; then mix in cinnamon. Add flour, a little at a time, stirring after each addition, and then beat well by hand for at least 2 minutes. Stir in baking soda quickly, and then mix (28 to 30 beats); immediately pour mixture into prepared pan. Using your hand, sprinkle topping over cake batter.

5. Bake 28 to 29 minutes, or until a cake tester inserted in center of cake comes out clean.

6. Remove pan from oven and place on a wire rack until cake is completely cooled. To store, cover cooled cake with plastic or place in an airtight container and refrigerate, or freeze.

Yield: One 13- by 9- by 2-inch cake (15 servings)

PER SERVING

Calories: 233.1   *Diabetic exchanges*
Protein: 4.4 g   *Starch:* 1
Fat: 11.2 g   *Fat:* 2
Carbohydrate: 29.7 g   *Fruit:* 1
Sodium: 241.1 mg

Pineapple-Orange Delight Crumb Cake

TOPPING

1½ cups unsweetened coconut,
2 tablespoons plus 2 teaspoons
   vegetable oil
2 tablespoons plus 2 teaspoons
   unsweetened orange juice
   concentrate (Minute Maid Reduced
   Acid)

1 teaspoon water
¼ cup chopped pecans

CAKE

¾ cup unsweetened diced pineapple
   tidbits, drained
2½ teaspoons grated orange rind
   (depending on personal taste, use
   additional ⅛ teaspoon)
6 egg whites or 3 extralarge eggs
⅓ cup plus 1¼ teaspoons vegetable oil
¾ cup plus 1 tablespoon unsweetened
   orange juice concentrate (Minute
   Maid Reduced Acid)

½ cup plus 3 tablespoons unsweetened
   apple juice concentrate (any
   brand)
2 cups plus 2 tablespoons all-purpose
   flour
2½ teaspoons baking soda

1. Preheat oven to 325°F. Grease and flour a 13- by 9- by 2-inch baking pan.

2. *To make topping:* In a medium-sized bowl, combine coconut with oil, concentrate, water, and nuts. Stir and set aside.

3. *To make batter:* Dice pineapple and measure out ¾ cup. Place pineapple in a

hand strainer and press lightly with a spoon to reduce moisture content. Set aside. Grate orange rind and set aside.

4. In a large bowl, combine eggs, oil, and concentrates. Beat for 1 minute using a hand-operated mechanical beater. Stir in pineapple and grated orange rind. Add flour, a little at a time, stirring, and then beat well by hand for at least 2 minutes. Stir in baking soda quickly, and then mix (28 to 30 beats); immediately pour mixture into prepared baking pan. Sprinkle coconut topping by hand over the top of the cake batter.

5. Bake 28 to 30 minutes, or until a cake tester inserted in center of cake comes out clean.

6. Remove pan from oven and place on a wire rack until cake is completely cooled. To store, cover cooled cake with plastic wrap or in an airtight container and store on countertop or freeze.

Yield: One 13- by 9- by 2-inch cake (15 servings)

PER SERVING

Calories: 260.3
Protein: 4.5 g
Fat: 14.3 g
Carbohydrate: 29.7 g

Sodium: 239.7 mg
Diabetic exchanges
  Starch: 2
  Fat: 3

Walnut-Raisin Cake

TOPPING

Generous ¼ cup finely chopped
    walnuts

Scant ¼ teaspoon cinnamon

CAKE

Very generous ½ cup chopped walnuts
Scant ⅓ cup minced raisins, packed
8 egg whites or 4 extralarge eggs
½ cup plus 2½ teaspoons vegetable oil
½ cup plus 2 tablespoons unsweetened
    apple juice concentrate (any brand)
½ cup plus 3 tablespoons unsweetened
    white grape juice concentrate
    (Welch's)

¾ cup unsweetened orange juice
    concentrate (Minute Maid
    Reduced Acid)
2½ teaspoons cinnamon
¼ teaspoon nutmeg
2¾ cups all-purpose flour
2½ teaspoons baking soda

1. Preheat oven to 325°F. Oil and flour a 13- by 9- by 2-inch baking pan.
2. *To make topping:* In a small bowl stir together nuts and cinnamon, set aside.
3. *To make cake:* Chop nuts and then mince raisins. Set these aside.
4. In a large bowl, combine eggs, oil, and concentrates. Beat for 1 minute with a hand-operated mechanical beater. Add cinnamon, nutmeg, and minced raisins and stir. Add flour a little at a time, stirring. Add nuts, and then beat well by hand for 2 minutes. Stir in baking soda quickly, and then mix (28 to 30 beats); immediately pour mixture into prepared baking pan. Sprinkle topping over batter.
5. Bake 30 minutes. Reduce heat to 300°F and continue baking for another 9 to 10 minutes, or until a cake tester inserted in center of cake comes out clean.
6. Remove pan from oven and place on a wire rack until cake is completely cooled. To store, cover cooled cake well with plastic wrap or in an airtight container and store on countertop or freeze.

Yield: One 13- by 9- by 2-inch cake (15 servings)

PER SERVING

Calories: 286.7
Protein: 6.3 g
Fat: 11.9 g
Carbohydrate: 39.6 g
Sodium: 247.1 mg

Diabetic exchanges
  Starch: 2
  Fat: 2
  Fruit: ½

WALNUT-RAISIN CAKE VARIATION: For a 9-inch square layer cake, pour batter into two generously oiled or greased and floured (or grease bottom and sides of pans and place waxed paper on pan bottoms) 9- by 9- by 2-inch square cake pans. Bake cake for about 28 minutes, or until a cake tester inserted in center of cake comes out clean. Remove pans from oven and place on a wire rack. Cool 10 minutes before loosening cake from sides of pans with a knife and removing cake from pan. Cool. Apply frosting of your choice between layers and on top. *Yield:* One 9-inch square layer cake.

CUPCAKE VARIATION: Follow the same instructions as for the cake, but fill 30 to 33 muffin cups with paper liners and reduce baking time to 19 to 20 minutes (at 325°F). Use a cake tester to test for doneness. When done, remove tins from oven and remove cupcakes to a table or wire rack to cool.

Apple-Banana Nut Cake

TOPPING

Generous ¼ cup chopped walnuts

Generous ¼ teaspoon cinnamon

CAKE

Very generous ½ cup chopped walnuts

Generous 1 cup mashed banana

⅓ cup vegetable oil

6 egg whites or 3 extralarge eggs

¾ cup unsweetened apple juice concentrate (any brand)

1 tablespoon unsweetened orange juice concentrate (Minute Maid Reduced Acid)

3 tablespoons plus 1 teaspoon water

Generous 2¼ to 2½ teaspoons cinnamon or to taste

2¼ cups all-purpose flour

2 teaspoons baking soda

1. Preheat oven to 325°F. Oil and flour a 13- by 9- by 2-inch baking pan.

2. *To make topping:* In a small bowl, stir together nuts and cinnamon and set aside.

3. *To make cake:* First, chop walnuts and set aside. In a large bowl, combine banana, oil, eggs, concentrates, and water. Beat mixture for 1 minute with a hand-operated mechanical beater. Add cinnamon and flour and beat well by hand. Add nuts and stir for 1 to 2 minutes. Stir in baking soda quickly, and then mix (28 to 30 beats); immediately pour batter into prepared baking pan. Sprinkle nut topping evenly over mixture.

4. Bake 26 to 28 minutes, or until a cake tester inserted in center of cake comes out clean.

5. Remove pan from oven and place on a wire rack until cake is completely cooled. To store, cover cooled cake with plastic wrap or in an airtight container and store on countertop or freeze.

Yield: One 13- by 9- by 2-inch cake (15 servings)

PER SERVING WITH TOPPING

Calories: 195.7

Protein: 5.1 g

Fat: 8.7 g

Carbohydrate: 25.2 g

Sodium: 194 mg

Diabetic exchanges

Starch: 1

Fat: 1½

Fruit: 1

Spice Cake

TOPPING

¼ cup finely chopped pecans

CAKE

¼ cup raisins, packed, minced
8 egg whites or 4 extralarge eggs
½ cup plus 1 tablespoon vegetable oil
½ cup plus 2 tablespoons unsweetened
   apple juice concentrate (any brand)
½ cup plus 3 tablespoons unsweetened
   white grape juice concentrate
   (Welch's)

¼ cup unsweetened orange juice
   concentrate (Minute Maid
   Reduced Acid)
2½ teaspoons cinnamon or to taste
2¾ cups all-purpose flour
2½ teaspoons baking soda

1. Preheat oven to 325°F. Oil and flour a 13- by 9- by 2-inch baking pan.

2. First mince raisins and set aside.

3. In a large bowl, combine eggs, oil, concentrates, and cinnamon. Beat for 1 minute with a hand-operated mechanical beater. Add minced raisins and stir. Add flour a little at a time, stirring, and then beat well by hand for 2 minutes. Stir in baking soda quickly, and then mix (28 to 30 beats); immediately pour mixture into prepared baking pan. Sprinkle chopped pecans on top.

4. Bake 30 minutes. Reduce heat to 300°F and continue baking for another 10 minutes, or until a cake tester inserted in center of cake comes out clean.

5. Remove pan from oven and place on a wire rack until cake is completely cooled. To store, cover cooled cake well with plastic wrap or in an airtight container and store on countertop or freeze.

Yield: One 13- by 9- by 2-inch cake (15 servings)

PER SERVING

Calories: 260.3
Protein: 4.9 g
Fat: 9.8 g
Carbohydrate: 38.4 g
Sodium: 246.9 mg

Diabetic exchanges
   Starch: 2
   Fat: 2
   Fruit: ½

LAYER-CAKE VARIATION: For a 9-inch square layer cake, pour batter into two generously oiled or greased and floured (or grease bottom and sides of pans and place waxed paper on pan bottoms) 9- by 9- by 2-inch square cake pans. Bake cake about 28 minutes or until a cake tester inserted in center of cake comes out clean. Remove pans from oven and place on a wire rack. Cool 10 minutes before loosening cake from sides of pans with a knife and removing cake from pan. Cool. Apply frosting of your choice between layers and on top. Yield: One 9-inch square layer cake.

CUPCAKE VARIATION: Follow the same instructions as for the cake, but fill 28 to 30 muffin cups with paper liners and reduce baking time to 19 to 20 minutes (at 325°F). Use a cake tester to test for doneness. When done, remove tins from oven and remove cupcakes to a table or wire rack to cool.

Apple Spice Cake

TOPPING

1 cup unsweetened coconut, premoistened with 1 tablespoon plus 2 teaspoons vegetable oil and 1 tablespoon plus 2 teaspoons unsweetened apple juice concentrate (any brand)

¼ cup chopped walnuts
Scant 1¼ cups peeled, cored, and diced apple
½ teaspoon cinnamon

CAKE

8 egg whites or 4 extralarge eggs
½ cup plus 1½ teaspoons vegetable oil
2 cups plus 1 tablespoon unsweetened apple juice concentrate (any brand)

2½ teaspoons cinnamon or to taste
2¾ cups all-purpose flour
2½ teaspoons baking soda

1. Preheat oven to 325°F. Oil and flour a 13- by 9- by 2-inch baking pan.
2. *To make topping:* In a medium-sized bowl, combine premoistened unsweetened coconut and chopped nuts. Stir and set aside. In a small bowl, combine apples and cinnamon. Stir and set aside.
3. In a large bowl, combine eggs, oil, concentrate, and cinnamon. Beat for 1 minute with a hand-operated mechanical beater.
4. Add flour to egg mixture a little at a time, stirring, and then beat well by hand for 2 full minutes. Stir in baking soda quickly, and then mix (28 to 30 beats); immediately pour mixture into prepared baking pan. Quickly sprinkle apples

evenly over top of batter, then quickly sprinkle coconut and nut mixture over top of apples.

5. Bake cake 30 minutes. Reduce heat to 300°F and continue baking for another 10 minutes, or until a cake tester inserted in center of cake comes out clean.

6. Remove pan from oven and place on a wire rack until cake is completely cooled. To store, cover cake well with plastic wrap or in an airtight container and refrigerate or freeze.

Yield: One 13- by 9- by 2-inch cake (15 servings)

PER SERVING

Calories: 294.8	*Diabetic exchanges*
Protein: 5.3 g	Starch: 2
Fat: 14.2 g	*Fat:* 3
Carbohydrate: 37.6 g	*Fruit:* ½
Sodium: 251.7 mg	

Golden Harvest Cake

¼ cup minced raisins, packed

1 cup grated carrot, packed

6 egg whites or 3 extralarge eggs

½ cup vegetable oil

¾ cup unsweetened apple juice
concentrate (any brand)

¼ cup plus 2 tablespoons unsweetened
orange juice concentrate (Minute
Maid Reduced Acid)

2 tablespoons water

2 teaspoons cinnamon

Scant ¼ teaspoon allspice

Scant 2½ cups all-purpose flour

2½ teaspoons baking soda

1. Preheat oven to 325°F. Oil and flour a 13- by 9- by 2-inch baking pan. Mince raisins; grate carrots; set aside.

2. In a large bowl, combine eggs, oil, concentrates, and water. Using a hand-operated mechanical beater, beat mixture until foamy—about 1 minute. Add cinnamon, allspice, raisins, carrot, and flour; beat by hand for 2 to 3 minutes. Stir in baking soda quickly, and then mix (28 to 30 beats); immediately pour mixture into prepared baking pan.

3. Bake 29 to 30 minutes, or until a cake tester inserted in center of cake comes out clean.

4. Remove pan from oven and place on a wire rack until cake is completely cooled. To store, place cooled cake in airtight container and store on countertop or freeze.

Yield: One 13- by 9- by 2-inch cake (15 servings)

PER SERVING

Calories: 193.7

Protein: 4.0 g

Fat: 7.6 g

Carbohydrate: 27.7 g

Sodium: 238.8 mg

Diabetic exchanges

  Starch: 1

  Fat: 1½

  Fruit: 1

GOLDEN HARVEST CUPCAKE VARIATION: This cake makes excellent cupcakes. Follow the same instructions as for the cake, but use 28 to 30 muffin cups with paper liners and reduce the baking time to 16 to 17 minutes (at 325°F). Use a cake tester to test for doneness. When done, remove tins from the oven and remove cupcakes to a table or wire rack to cool.

GOLDEN HARVEST LAYER-CAKE VARIATION: For a 9-inch round layer cake, pour batter into two generously oiled or greased and floured (or grease bottom and sides of pans and place waxed paper on pan bottoms) 9-inch round cake pans. Bake at 325°F for 21 to 23 minutes, or until a cake tester inserted in center of cake comes out clean. Remove pans from oven and place on a wire rack. Cool 10 minutes before loosening cake from sides of pans with a knife and removing cake from pans. Cool. Apply frosting of your choice between layers and on top.

Orange-Carrot Cake

6 egg whites or 3 extralarge eggs
½ cup vegetable oil
½ cup plus 3 tablespoons unsweetened apple juice concentrate (any brand)
½ cup plus 1 tablespoon unsweetened orange juice concentrate (Minute Maid Reduced Acid)

Scant 2¾ teaspoons cinnamon or to taste
1½ cups packed grated carrot
Scant 2½ cups all-purpose flour, tapped lightly 4 to 5 times
2½ teaspoons baking soda

1. Preheat oven to 325°F. Oil and flour a 13- by 9- by 2-inch baking pan.
2. In a large bowl, combine eggs, oil, and concentrates. Using a hand-operated mechanical beater, beat mixture until foamy—about 1 minute. Add cinnamon, carrot, and flour; beat by hand for 2 minutes. Stir in baking soda quickly, and then mix (28 to 30 beats); immediately pour mixture into prepared baking pan.
3. Bake 32 to 33 minutes, or until a cake tester inserted in center of cake comes out clean.
4. Remove pan from oven and place on a wire rack until cake is completely cooled. To store, place cooled cake in an airtight container and store on a countertop or freeze.

Yield: One 13- by 9- by 2-inch cake (15 servings)

PER SERVING

Calories: 190.9   *Diabetic exchanges*
Protein: 4.0 g   *Starch:* 1
Fat: 7.6 g   *Fat:* 1½
Carbohydrate: 26.8 g   *Fruit:* 1
Sodium: 239.6 mg

CUPCAKE VARIATION: This cake is very moist and therefore makes excellent cupcakes. Follow the same instructions as for the cake, but use 28 to 30 muffin cups with paper liners and reduce the baking time to 18 to 20 minutes (at 325°F). Use a cake tester to test for doneness. When done, remove tins from oven and remove cupcakes to a table or wire rack to cool.

LAYER-CAKE VARIATION: For a 9-inch round layer cake, pour batter into two generously oiled or greased and floured (or grease bottom and sides of pans and place waxed paper on pan bottoms) 9-inch round cake pans. Bake at 325°F for 24 to 27 minutes, or until a cake tester inserted in center of cake comes out clean. Remove pans from oven and place on a wire rack. Cool 10 minutes before loosening cake from sides of pans with a knife and removing cake from pans. Cool. Apply frosting of your choice between layers and on top.

Apple-Orange Poppy Seed Cake

By changing the amount and kind of concentrate, this cake can be made two different ways, each with its own wonderful flavor (see *Apple Variation*).

8 egg whites or 4 extralarge eggs
½ cup plus 1½ teaspoons vegetable oil
1¼ cups unsweetened apple juice
   concentrate (any brand)
¾ cup plus 1 tablespoon unsweetened
   orange juice concentrate (Minute
   Maid Reduced Acid)

1 tablespoon plus 2 teaspoons poppy
   seeds (optional), divided
1½ teaspoons cinnamon
2¾ cups all-purpose flour
2½ teaspoons baking soda

1. Preheat oven to 325°F. Oil and flour a 13- by 9- by 2-inch baking pan.

2. In a large bowl, combine eggs, oil, and concentrates, 1 tablespoon poppy seeds, and cinnamon. Beat for 1 minute with a hand-operated mechanical beater. Add flour a little at a time, stirring, and beat well by hand for 2 minutes. Stir in baking soda quickly, and then mix (28 to 30 beats); immediately pour mixture into prepared baking pan. Sprinkle remaining poppy seeds on top.

3. Bake 30 minutes. Reduce heat to 300°F and continue baking for another 10 minutes, or until cake tester inserted in center of cake comes out clean.

4. Remove pan from oven and place on a wire rack until cake is completely cooled. To store, cover cooled cake well with plastic wrap or in an airtight container and store on countertop or freeze.

Yield: One 13- by 9- by 2-inch cake (15 servings)

PER SERVING (WITH 1 TABLESPOON POPPY SEEDS)

Calories: 227.7
Protein: 4.8 g
Fat: 8.3 g
Carbohydrate: 33.5 g
Sodium: 245.9

Diabetic exchanges
Starch: 1½
Fat: 1½
Fruit: 1

APPLE VARIATION: For a mild apple flavor, substitute 2 cups plus 1 tablespoon unsweetened apple juice concentrate for the apple and orange juice concentrates.

CUPCAKE VARIATION: Fill 28 to 30 muffin cups with paper liners and reduce the baking time to 19 to 20 minutes (at 325°F). Use a cake tester to test for doneness. When done, remove tins from oven and remove cupcakes to a table or rack to cool.

LAYER-CAKE VARIATION: For a 9-inch square layer cake, pour batter into two generously oiled or greased and floured 9- by 9- by 2-inch square cake pans. Bake about 28 minutes, or until a cake tester inserted in center of cake comes out clean. Remove pan from oven and place on a wire rack. Cool 10 minutes before loosening cake from sides of pan with knife and removing cake from pan. Cool. Apply frosting of your choice between layers and on top. Yield: One 9-inch square layer cake.

Apple-Potato Layer Cake

Gluten-Free
Contains Egg Yolks; Not Cholesterol-Free

1 cup Ener-G Brand Potato Mix (contains corn-free baking powder)	¼ teaspoon plus ⅛ teaspoon cinnamon
½ cup plus 2 tablespoons plus 2½ teaspoons unsweetened apple juice concentrate (any brand)	½ teaspoon vanilla
	Generous ¼ cup vegetable oil
	1 extralarge egg
	1 teaspoon baking soda

1. Preheat oven to 350°F. Oil an 8½-inch round cake pan. Using a small-sized bowl, measure out Potato Mix. Set aside. Combine concentrate, cinnamon, vanilla, and oil in a small bowl; set aside.

2. Separate egg by placing the yolk in a medium-sized bowl and the egg white in a small-sized bowl. Using a hand-operated mechanical beater, beat egg white until very stiff. It should not fall out of the bowl when the bowl is turned upside down.

3. Quickly add concentrate mixture and baking soda to egg yolk. Beat ingredients with a hand-operated mechanical beater for 30 seconds. Quickly add Potato Mix, half of mix at a time, stirring after each addition. Immediately fold in stiff egg white.

4. Bake 23 to 24 minutes, or until a cake tester inserted in center of cake comes out clean.

5. Remove baking pan from oven and place on a wire rack. Cool cake for 10 minutes, cut around sides with a knife, and turn cake out onto wire rack to cool. (You may have to hit bottom of cake pan to loosen cake.) While cake is cooling, you can make the Apple Topping and Filling (see page 76).

6. When cake has cooled, cut cake horizontally, remove top layer, and set aside.

Place bottom layer on a serving plate and spread with half the warm Apple Topping and Filling. Replace top layer and spread with warm Apple Topping and Filling. To store, cover cake with aluminum foil and refrigerate or freeze. This cake tends to dry out quickly.

Yield: One 8½-inch layer cake (8 Servings)

PER SERVING (WITHOUT APPLE TOPPING OR FILLING)

Calories: 179.9
Protein: 1.4 g
Fat: 7.6 g
Carbohydrate: 26.9 g
Sodium: 224.9 mg

Diabetic exchanges
   Starch: 1
   Fat: 1½
   Fruit: 1

Apple Topping and Filling

2 cups peeled, cored, and diced apples
¼ teaspoon cinnamon
1 tablespoon vegetable oil
2 tablespoons plus 1½ teaspoons
   unsweetened apple juice
   concentrate (any brand)

¼ cup water
2 tablespoons Ener-G Brand pure
   potato starch flour

1. In a medium-sized saucepan, place apples, cinnamon, oil, concentrate, and water. Simmer ingredients on medium-low heat for 15 to 20 minutes, stirring often, until fruit is soft. Remove saucepan from stove and set aside to cool until lukewarm.

2. Add potato starch flour to lukewarm apple mixture. Stir until well combined. Place saucepan back on stove and cook on low heat, stirring all the time, until filling thickens. Spread filling on cake while filling is still warm.

Yield: Enough topping and filling for one 8½-inch cake (8 servings)

PER SERVING

Calories: 49
Protein: 0.1 g
Fat: 1.8 g
Carbohydrate: 8.6 g

Sodium: 1.8 mg
Diabetic exchanges
  Fat: ½
  Fruit: ½

Quick Apple Upside-Down Cake

TOPPING

3 cups peeled, cored, and diced
   McIntosh apples

1 tablespoon vegetable oil
Scant 1 teaspoon cinnamon

CAKE

2 egg whites *or* 1 extralarge egg
¼ cup vegetable oil
½ teaspoon cinnamon
¾ cup unsweetened apple juice
   concentrate (any brand)

1½ cups all-purpose flour
1¼ teaspoons baking soda

1. Preheat oven to 350°F. Oil an 8- by 8- by 2-inch glass baking dish.

2. *To prepare topping:* In a large bowl, toss together apples, oil, and cinnamon. Spread mixture evenly into prepared baking dish.

3. In a large bowl, combine egg, oil, cinnamon, and concentrate; beat well by hand. Add flour and beat for 2 minutes by hand. Stir in baking soda quickly, and then mix (28 to 30 beats); immediately pour over apple mixture.

4. Bake 30 minutes at 350°F. Turn down oven to 325°F and bake 5 minutes more, or until a cake tester inserted in center of cake comes out clean.

5. Remove baking dish from oven and place on a wire rack. Cool 20 minutes before loosening cake with a knife. Invert cake onto serving platter. Serve warm or cold. To store, place cooled cake in an airtight container and refrigerate or freeze.

Yield: One 8- by 8- by 2-inch cake (9 servings)

PER SERVING

Calories: 207.3
Protein: 3.1 g
Fat: 8 g
Carbohydrate: 31.3 g
Sodium: 193.4 mg

Diabetic exchanges
   Starch: 1
   Fat: 1½
   Fruit: 1

Apple Upside-Down Cake

No Egg

TOPPING

3 cups peeled, cored, and diced
McIntosh apples

1 tablespoon vegetable oil

1 teaspoon cinnamon

CAKE

¼ cup vegetable oil

½ teaspoon cinnamon

¼ cup unsweetened apple juice
concentrate (any brand)

½ cup plus 2 tablespoons water

1½ teaspoons pure potato-starch flour

1½ cups plus 1 tablespoon all-purpose
flour

2 tablespoons water

1½ teaspoons egg replacer (Ener-G
brand)

1 teaspoon baking soda

2½ teaspoons baking powder

1. Preheat oven to 350°F. Oil an 8- by 8- by 2-inch glass baking dish.

2. *To prepare topping:* In a large bowl, toss together apples, oil, and cinnamon. Spread mixture evenly into prepared baking dish.

3. In a large bowl, combine oil, cinnamon, concentrate, water, and potato-starch flour; beat well. Add flour and beat for 2 minutes by hand.

4. In a small bowl, and using a hand-operated mechanical beater, beat together water and egg replacer until bubbles form (mixture should not be thick or stiff). Pour egg-replacer mixture into flour-and-concentrate mixture and stir for 20 seconds by hand. Stir in baking soda and baking powder quickly, and then mix (28 to 30 beats); immediately pour mixture evenly over apple mixture.

5. Bake 30 minutes at 350°F. Turn oven down to 325°F and bake another 5 minutes, or until a cake tester inserted in center of cake comes out clean.

6. Remove baking dish from oven and place on a wire rack. Cool 25 minutes before loosening cake with a knife. Invert cake onto serving platter. Serve warm or cold. To store, place cooled cake in an airtight container and refrigerate or freeze.

Yield: One 8- by 8- by 2-inch cake (9 servings)

PER SERVING

Calories: 186
Protein: 2.3 g
Fat: 7.9 g
Carbohydrate: 26.7 g
Sodium: 186.6 mg

Diabetic exchanges
  Starch: 1
  Fat: 1½
  Fruit: ¾

Pineapple-Cherry Upside-Down Cake

TOPPING

One 20-ounce can Dole unsweetened
  pineapple slices plus juice from the
  can
3 to 4 more Dole pineapple slices from
  a second can
26 unsweetened, frozen, and thawed
  dark sweet cherries

½ cup unsweetened apple juice
  concentrate (any brand)
1 teaspoon water
3 tablespoons arrowroot or cornstarch

CAKE

2¼ cups all-purpose flour
1 cup date sugar, tapped well
1 tablespoon soy powder, dry milk
  powder, or all-purpose flour
⅔ cup vegetable oil
1 tablespoon water
1¼ cups unsweetened apple juice
  concentrate (any brand)

½ teaspoon cinnamon
5 dashes of nutmeg
8 egg whites *or* 4 extralarge eggs,
  beaten until quite foamy
2 teaspoons baking soda

1. Preheat oven to 325°F. Oil sides and bottoms of two 8- by 8- by 2-inch glass or ceramic baking dishes. Add 1 tablespoon more oil to the bottom of *each* dish and tip dish so the oil covers bottom evenly.

2. *To prepare topping:* Drain pineapple slices (reserving juice) and pat dry. Place thawed cherries on a paper towel and pat dry. Arrange pineapple slices in the bottoms of the baking dishes and place cherries in the centers of the pineapple rings and in between them.

3. In a small saucepan, combine concentrate, the juice from the can of pineapple,

the water, and arrowroot. Heat, stirring constantly, over medium heat until mixture thickens. Remove mixture from heat and let cool.

4. When mixture is cool, spread it over arranged pineapple rings and cherries. Set aside.

5. *To prepare cake:* In a large bowl, stir together flour, date sugar, soy powder (or dry milk or flour), oil, water, and concentrate. Add cinnamon, nutmeg, and eggs and beat well by hand for 2 to 3 minutes. Stir in baking soda quickly, and then mix (28 to 30 beats); immediately pour batter over topping, dividing batter equally between the two baking dishes.

6. Bake 30 minutes at 325°F. Reduce oven to 300°F and continue baking 10 to 12 minutes, or until a cake tester inserted in center of cake comes out clean.

7. Remove baking dishes from oven and place on wire racks. Cool 1 minute before loosening cakes with a knife. Invert cakes onto serving plates. Serve warm or cold. To store, place cooled cakes in airtight containers and refrigerate or freeze.

Yield: Two 8- by 8- by 2-inch cakes (18 servings)

PER SERVING

Calories: 241	*Diabetic exchanges*
Protein: 3.5 g	Starch: 1½
Fat: 8.4 g	Fat: 1½
Carbohydrate: 38 g	Fruit: 1
Sodium: 171.4 mg	

CUPCAKE VARIATION: This cake is very moist and therefore makes excellent cupcakes—except that you won't be using the topping. Follow the same instructions for the cake, beginning at step 5. Preheat the oven to 325°F, fill 24 muffin cups with paper liners, and reduce the total baking time to only 16 to 18 minutes. Use a cake tester to test for doneness. When done, remove tins from oven and remove cupcakes to a table or wire rack to cool.

LAYER-CAKE VARIATIONS: For this layer cake, you won't be using the topping. Follow the same instructions for the cake, beginning at step 5. Preheat the oven to 325°F.

For an 8- by 8- by 2-inch layer cake, generously oil two 8- by 8- by 2-inch glass or ceramic baking dishes. Bake 28 to 30 minutes, or until a cake tester inserted in center of cake comes out clean. Remove baking dishes from oven and place on a wire rack. Cool 10 minutes before loosening cakes from sides of dishes with a knife and inverting cakes from dishes. Cool. Apply frosting of your choice between layers and on top.

For a 9-inch round layer cake, pour batter into two generously oiled or greased (or grease bottom and sides of pans and place waxed paper on pan bottoms) 9-inch round cake pans. Bake at 325°F for 31 to 33 minutes, or until a cake tester inserted in center of cake comes out clean. Remove pans from oven and place on a wire rack. Cool 10 minutes before loosening cakes from sides of pans with a knife and inverting cakes from pans. Cool. Apply frosting of your choice between layers and on top.

FRUIT PIES

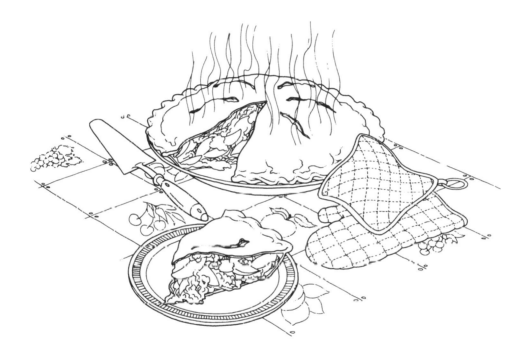

Because of their natural sweetness, apples, pears, peaches, pineapples, rhubarb, cherries, and blueberries all make delicious pie fillings. Try to use fresh fruit whenever possible, though frozen fruit works just as well if you are careful to drain it.

Of course, the secret to an outstanding pie is its crust. This chapter contains many different recipes for crusts, and I hope that from among them you will find at least one that works for you. Here are some hints that you may find useful in turning out the "perfect" pie:

- Make sure you drain the fruit well so that the filling does not become soggy.
- You may use a bit more or less of each fruit concentrate, depending on your taste. Three ounces of concentrate will result in a not-so-sweet pie; five or six ounces will result in a sweet pie. Just remember that if you use more concentrate than called for in a recipe, you may need to add more tapioca as a thickener.
- Pie crusts will be lighter and tenderer if you keep the dough cold until just before it goes in the oven. For this reason, I usually prepare the fruit filling first, then the topping (if I'm using a crumb-crust topping instead of a top crust), and finally the crust.
- Always grease your pie plates so that the crust does not stick to the bottom.
- Always cool pies thoroughly before storing them uncovered in the refrigerator, or cover and place them in the freezer.

Crust for a Double-Crust Pie

⅔ cup vegetable shortening of choice
   or cold lard with no preservatives or
   additives

2 cups all-purpose flour
1 teaspoon salt
4 to 7 tablespoons ice water

1. In a medium-sized bowl, combine shortening, flour, and salt. Using a fork or pastry cutter, cut up mixture until it resembles small peas.

2. Add ice water a little at a time, stirring gently with a fork until a soft dough ball is formed (see *Note*).

3. Cover dough and refrigerate until ready to use. (Be sure to use dough within 45 minutes to 1 hour.)

Yield: Enough dough for one 9-inch, double-crust pie (8 servings)

PER SERVING

Calories: 260
Protein: 3.3 g
Fat: 16.8 g
Carbohydrate: 23.8 g

Sodium: 244.9 mg
Diabetic exchanges
  Starch: 1½
  Fat: 3

Note: Recipe can be doubled, tripled, or quadrupled if making more than one pie. If you increase the recipe, do not make one large dough ball in step 2. Instead, make one dough ball for each crust by mixing the ice water with about 2 cups of the shortening/flour/salt mixture at a time. This allows you to handle the dough as little as possible, which helps keep the crust flaky and light.

Extra-Rich Crust for a Double-Crust Pie

¾ cup vegetable shortening   1 teaspoon salt
2 cups all-purpose flour   About 5 tablespoons ice water

1. In a medium-sized bowl, combine shortening, flour, and salt. Using a fork or pastry cutter, cut up mixture until it resembles small peas.

2. Add ice water a little at a time, stirring gently with a fork until a soft dough ball is formed.

3. Cover dough and refrigerate until ready to use. (Be sure to use dough within 45 minutes to 1 hour.)

Yield: Enough dough for one 9-inch, double-crust pie (8 servings)

PER SERVING

Calories: 283.7   *Sodium:* 267.1 mg
Protein: 3.2 g   *Diabetic exchanges*
Fat: 19.5 g   *Starch:* 1½
Carbohydrate: 23.8 g   *Fat:* 4

Oil-Based Crust for a 9-Inch, Single-Crust Pie

1 cup all-purpose flour
Scant 3 tablespoons raw wheat germ
½ teaspoon salt

¼ cup plus 1 tablespoon plus ½ teaspoon vegetable oil
2 tablespoons cold water

1. In a medium-sized bowl, stir together flour, wheat germ, and salt.
2. In a small bowl, stir together oil and water.
3. Pour liquid mixture over dry mixture and stir with a fork to form a soft dough.
4. Place dough on a sheet of waxed paper and flatten slightly with your hand. Cover dough with a second sheet of waxed paper and roll out dough to desired thickness of crust. Peel off top paper, turn dough over into an oiled 9-inch pie plate, and peel off second sheet of paper. Gently press dough into pie plate, fixing any rips and holes.
5. Add pie filling of choice. Add topping of choice (see pages 122–134) and bake according to directions for pie filling.

Yield: Enough dough for one 9-inch, single-crust pie (8 servings)

PER SERVING

Calories: 145
Protein: 2.4 g
Fat: 9.2 g
Carbohydrate: 13.2 g

Sodium: 122.5 mg
Diabetic exchanges
   Starch: ¾
   Fat: 2

Oil-Based Crust for a 9-Inch, Double-Crust Pie

2 cups all-purpose flour
Scant 6 tablespoons raw wheat germ
1 teaspoon salt

Scant ⅔ cup vegetable oil
4 tablespoons cold water

1. In a medium-sized bowl, stir together flour, wheat germ, and salt.

2. In a small bowl, stir together oil and water.

3. Pour liquid mixture over dry mixture and stir with a fork to form a soft dough. Divide dough in half.

4. Place one ball of dough on a sheet of waxed paper and flatten slightly with your hand. Cover dough with a second sheet of waxed paper and roll out to desired thickness of crust. Peel off top paper, turn dough over into an oiled 9-inch pie plate, and peel off second sheet of paper. Gently press dough into pie plate, fixing any rips and holes.

5. Add pie filling of choice. Flatten and roll out second half of dough as above. Place dough over pie filling, mending any rips and holes as best you can. Pinch layers together around edges and flute. Bake according to directions for pie filling.

Yield: Enough dough for one 9-inch, double-crust pie (8 servings)

PER SERVING

Calories: 274
Protein: 4.8 g
Fat: 16.5 g
Carbohydrate: 26.4 g

Sodium: 245.1 mg
Diabetic exchanges
  Starch: 1¾
  Fat: 3

Spelt Oil-Based Crust for a 9-Inch, Single-Crust Pie

Has Gluten

For a double-crust pie, just double this recipe.

1 cup plus 3 tablespoons spelt flour,
  tapped well
½ teaspoon salt

4 tablespoons vegetable oil
2 tablespoons plus 1 teaspoon cold
  water

1. In a medium-sized bowl, stir together flour and salt.
2. In a small bowl, stir together oil and water.
3. Pour liquid mixture over dry mixture and stir with a fork to form a soft dough. If dough is too dry, add a little more water.
4. Place dough on a sheet of waxed paper and flatten slightly with your hand. Cover dough with a second sheet of waxed paper and roll out dough to desired thickness of crust. Peel off top paper, turn dough over into an oiled 9-inch pie plate, and peel off second sheet of paper. Gently press dough into pie plate, fixing any rips and holes.
5. Add pie filling of choice. Add topping of choice (see pages 122–134) and bake according to directions for pie filling.

Yield: Enough dough for one 9-inch, single-crust pie (8 servings)

PER SERVING

Calories: 125.5
Protein: 3 g
Fat: 7.4 g
Carbohydrate: 13.7 g

Sodium: 133.2 mg
Diabetic exchanges
  Starch: 1
  Fat: 1½

Barley-Rice Pie Crust

1 cup barley flour
½ cup white-rice flour
½ teaspoon salt

3 tablespoons plus 1½ teaspoons
    vegetable shortening or lard
¼ cup plus 1 teaspoon water

1. Preheat oven to 350°F. Oil a 9-inch pie plate.

2. In a medium-sized bowl, stir together barley flour, rice flour, and salt. Add shortening and cut into flour mixture using a pastry cutter or a fork. Add water and mix well; mixture will be dry.

3. Pat dough into an oiled 9-inch pie plate. Make sure dough covers sides and bottom evenly. Press pastry to make edge. Add pie filling of choice. Place a crumb-crust topping (Barley-Rice Topping, page 125, is very good) over fruit and bake according to directions for pie filling.

Yield: One 9-inch pie crust (8 servings)

PER SERVING

Calories: 120
Protein: 2 g
Fat: 5.5 g
Carbohydrate: 16.4 g

Sodium: 170.2 g
Diabetic exchanges
  Starch: 1
  Fat: 1

Oatmeal Crust

1¼ cups oat flour
Generous ¼ teaspoon salt
2 tablespoons vegetable oil
4 to 4½ tablespoons water

1. Preheat oven to 350°F. Oil a 9-inch pie plate.

2. In a medium-sized bowl, stir together all ingredients with a fork.

3. Pat dough into prepared pie plate. Press pastry between fingers to make an edge. Add pie filling of choice; place a crumb-crust topping (see pages 122–134) over fruit and bake according to directions for pie filling.

4. If baking pie crust alone, use fork to prick bottom in several places to prevent buckling. Bake 18 to 20 minutes, or until crust is golden.

Yield: One 9-inch pie crust (8 servings)

PER SERVING

Calories: 93	*Sodium:* 61.5 mg
Protein: 2.7 g	*Diabetic exchanges*
Fat: 4.3 g	*Starch:* ¾
Carbohydrate: 11.6 g	*Fat:* ¾

Amaranth Pie Crust

Gluten-Free

¾ cup amaranth flour
¾ teaspoon homemade baking powder
½ teaspoon salt

2 tablespoons plus 2 teaspoons
  vegetable oil
3 tablespoons cold water

1. In a medium-sized bowl, stir together flour, baking powder, and salt; set aside.
2. In a small bowl, stir together oil and water.
3. Pour liquid mixture over dry mixture and stir with a fork to form a soft dough.
4. Place dough into an oiled 9-inch pie plate. Press the dough over bottom and sides evenly, pressing dough into a thin crust.
5. Add pie filling of choice. Add topping of choice (see pages 122–134) and bake according to directions for pie filling.

Yield: Enough dough for one 9-inch, single-crust pie (8 servings)

PER SERVING

Calories: 82.1	*Sodium:* 133.2 mg
Protein: 1.5 g	*Diabetic exchanges*
Fat: 5.1 g	*Starch:* ½
Carbohydrate: 7.3 g	*Fat:* 1

Prebaked Shortening-Based Brown Rice Pie Crust

Gluten-Free

1 cup brown rice flour	⅓ cup vegetable shortening
¼ teaspoon salt	¼ cup cold water
1 teaspoon guar gum	

1. Preheat oven to 350°F. Oil a 9-inch pie plate.

2. In a medium-sized bowl, stir together flour, salt, and gum, using a large metal spoon. Add shortening and, using a fork or pastry cutter, work shortening into rice flour mixture until blended together well.

3. Add water a little at a time, stirring gently with a large metal spoon to moisten all ingredients. Using your hands, form mixture into a large, soft ball of dough. Break off an inch-sized ball of dough and press into side of pie plate. Repeat with more balls until side of pan is covered; repeat procedure to form bottom. When pie plate is covered, go over again, pressing and working the dough to form a smooth crust. Make a narrow ridge around top of pie shell to finish off edge.

4. Bake 17 to 18 minutes, or until crust looks dry (see *Note*). You can also check by tapping a fork lightly on bottom of crust. It should sound crisp. Do not overbake or the crust will be too dry. Small cracks in crust are normal.

5. Remove pie plate from oven and place on a wire rack to cool for at least 30 minutes before filling.

6. Prepare pie filling of choice. Cook filling on top of stove until fruit is soft. Pour partially cooled filling into prebaked, cooled pie shell.

Yield: Enough dough for one 9-inch, single-crust pie (8 servings)

PER SERVING

Calories: 147.8	*Sodium:* 68.6 mg
Protein: 1.5 g	*Diabetic exchanges*
Fat: 9.1 g	*Starch:* 1
Carbohydrate: 15.4 g	*Fat:* 2

Note: You can also prebake brown rice pie crust for 10 minutes, then add pie filling of choice into shell, add topping of choice, and bake according to directions for pie filling.

Prebaked Oil-Based Brown Rice Pie Crust

Gluten-Free

1 cup plus 2 tablespoons brown rice flour

Generous ¼ teaspoon salt

2 tablespoons vegetable oil

¼ cup plus 1 tablespoon plus 2 teaspoons cold water

1. Preheat oven to 350°F. Oil a 9-inch pie plate.

2. In a medium-sized bowl, stir together flour and salt, using a large metal spoon. Set aside.

3. In a small bowl, using a hand-operated mechanical beater, beat together oil and water. Scraping sides of bowl well, pour liquid mixture over dry flour mixture. Stir and mix well with a large metal spoon to distribute moisture evenly to form a moist, crumbly dough.

4. Transfer to prepared pie plate by gently patting out only small amounts of dough at a time. Do this evenly, working around side of pie plate; repeat with small amounts of dough over bottom. When pie plate is covered, go over again, pressing and working the dough to form a smooth crust. Form a narrow edge around top to finish off pie shell.

5. Bake 15 to 16 minutes, or until crust looks dry or crust on bottom sounds crisp when tapped with a fork (see *Note*). Small cracks in crust are normal. Do not overbake or crust will be too dry.

6. Remove pie plate from oven and place on a wire rack to cool for at least 30 minutes before filling.

7. Prepare pie filling of choice. Cook filling on top of stove until fruit is soft. Pour partially cooled filling into prebaked, cooled pie shell.

Yield: Enough dough for one 9-inch, single-crust pie (8 servings)

PER SERVING

Calories: 110.8
Protein: 1.6 g
Fat: 4 g
Carbohydrate: 17 g

Sodium: 68.4 mg
Diabetic exchanges
  Starch: 1
  Fat: 1

Note: You can also prebake brown rice pie crust for 9 to 10 minutes, then add pie filling of choice into shell, add topping of choice, and bake according to directions for pie filling.

Mixed Granola Pie Crust

1¼ cups rolled oats

½ cup all-purpose flour or oat flour

⅔ cup unsweetened coconut,
    premoistened with 2 teaspoons
    water and 2 teaspoons vegetable oil

⅔ cup chopped nuts

Scant ¼ cup sesame seeds

2 teaspoons poppy seeds

½ teaspoon cinnamon

3 tablespoons sunflower seeds

7 tablespoons vegetable oil

1. Oil a 10-inch pie plate.

2. In a large bowl, stir together all ingredients with a fork. Set aside 1 cup (packed) of mixture for topping.

3. Press remaining mixture into bottom of prepared pie plate. Spread mixture over bottom and sides of plate, pressing firmly. Add pie filling of choice. Sprinkle 1 cup of reserved mixture over top of pie filling. Bake according to directions for pie filling.

Yield: One 10-inch pie crust plus topping (8 servings)

PER SERVING (USING PECANS FOR CHOPPED NUTS)

Calories: 315

Protein: 5.2 g

Fat: 26.9 g

Carbohydrate: 16.9 g

Sodium: 3.1 mg

Diabetic exchanges

   Starch: 1

   Fat: 5

Teff Pie Crust

Has Gluten

1 cup teff flour
⅛ teaspoon salt

¼ cup vegetable oil
¼ cup cold water

1. Place flour in a medium-sized bowl.
2. In a small bowl, stir together salt, oil, and water.
3. Pour liquid over flour and stir with a fork to form dough.
4. Pat and press dough into an oiled 9-inch pie plate. Make sure dough covers sides and bottom evenly. Add pie filling of choice. Place a crumb-crust topping over fruit and bake 45 to 50 minutes, or according to directions for pie filling.

Yield: One 9-inch pie crust (8 servings)

PER SERVING

Calories: 130
Protein: 2.5 g
Fat: 7.3 g
Carbohydrate: 14.5 g

Sodium: 35.8 mg
Diabetic exchanges
  Starch: 1
  Fat: 1½

Note: For a prebaked pie crust, use fork to prick bottom and sides in several places to prevent buckling. Bake 12 to 15 minutes, or until crust is no longer damp, but dry looking.

Apple or Pear Pie

4 cups peeled, cored, and sliced apples
  or pears
½ teaspoon cinnamon
2 to 2½ tablespoons Minute tapioca
2 tablespoons vegetable shortening,
  vegetable oil, or lard

½ to ¾ cup unsweetened apple juice
  concentrate (any brand)
One 9-inch pie shell of choice (see
  pages 85–95) plus top crust or
  topping of choice (see pages
  122–134)

1. Preheat oven to 350°F.

2. In a large bowl, stir together fruit, cinnamon, tapioca, shortening, and concentrate; allow mixture to sit for 10 minutes. Pour mixture into pie shell of choice and add topping or crust of choice.

3. Bake 50 to 55 minutes, or until topping or crust is golden.

4. Remove pie from oven and place on a wire rack to cool. Serve warm or cold. To store, place cooled pie uncovered in refrigerator or place in an airtight container and freeze.

Yield: One 9-inch pie (8 servings)

PER SERVING (FILLING ONLY)

Calories: 99.2
Protein: 0.2 g
Fat: 3.4 g
Carbohydrate: 18 g

Sodium: 4.4 mg
Diabetic exchanges
  Fat: ½
  Fruit: 1

Blueberry Pie

Two 16-ounce packages frozen
   blueberries, thawed and drained
⅓ cup peeled, pitted, and sliced
   peaches (*do not pack*)
2 tablespoons vegetable oil
2 tablespoons water

2 tablespoons Minute tapioca
¼ teaspoon lemon juice
One 9-inch pie shell of choice (see
   pages 85–95) plus top crust or
   topping of choice (see pages
   122–134)

1. Preheat oven to 450°F.

2. Puree ½ cup blueberries, the peaches, oil, and water in a blender. In a large bowl, stir together fruit puree, remaining blueberries, tapioca, and lemon juice; allow mixture to sit for 10 to 15 minutes. Pour mixture into pie shell of choice and add topping or crust of choice.

3. Bake at 450°F for 15 minutes. Reduce oven to 350°F and continue baking for 35 minutes, or until topping or crust is golden.

4. Remove pie plate from oven and place on a wire rack to cool. Serve warm or cold. To store, place cooled pie uncovered in refrigerator or place in an airtight container and freeze.

Yield: One 9-inch pie (8 servings)

PER SERVING (FILLING ONLY)

Calories: 111
Protein: 0.8 g
Fat: 4.3 g
Carbohydrate: 19.8 g

Sodium: 7.1 mg
Diabetic exchanges
   Fat: ¾
   Fruit: 1⅓

Blueberry-Prune Pie

⅓ cup sliced peaches (*do not pack*)
10 pitted prunes (medium)
2 tablespoons water
1½ tablespoons vegetable oil
Two 16-ounce packages blueberries, thawed and drained

2 tablespoons Minute tapioca
One 9-inch pie shell of choice (see pages 85–95) plus top crust or topping of choice (see pages 122–134)

1. Preheat oven to 450°F.

2. Puree peaches, prunes, water, and oil in a blender.

3. In a large bowl, stir together fruit puree, blueberries, and tapioca; allow mixture to sit for 10 minutes. Pour mixture into pie shell of choice and add topping or crust of choice.

4. Bake at 450°F for 15 minutes. Reduce oven to 350°F and continue baking for 35 minutes, or until topping or crust is golden.

5. Remove pie plate from oven and place on a wire rack to cool. Serve warm or cold. To store, place cooled pie uncovered in refrigerator or place in an airtight container and freeze.

Yield: One 9-inch pie (8 servings)

PER SERVING (FILLING ONLY)

Calories: 131
Protein: 1.1 g
Fat: 3.4 g
Carbohydrate: 27.1 g

Sodium: 7.6 mg
Diabetic exchanges
  Fat: ¾
  Fruit: 1¾

Cherry-Peach Pie

Two 16-ounce packages frozen dark
    sweet cherries, thawed and
    drained
½ cup peeled, pitted, and sliced
    peaches, patted dry (*do not pack*)
2 tablespoons unsweetened apple juice
    concentrate (any brand)

2 tablespoons vegetable oil
¼ teaspoon lemon juice
1½ to 2 tablespoons Minute tapioca
One 9-inch pie shell of choice (see
    pages 85–95) plus top crust or
    topping of choice (see pages
    122–134)

1. Preheat oven to 450°F.

2. Puree 12 of the cherries, the peaches, concentrate, and oil in a blender. In a large bowl, stir together fruit puree, remaining cherries, lemon juice, and tapioca; allow mixture to sit for 10 minutes. Pour mixture into pie shell of choice and add topping or crust of choice.

3. Bake at 450°F for 15 minutes. Reduce oven to 350°F and continue baking for 35 minutes, or until topping or crust is golden.

4. Remove pie plate from oven and place on a wire rack to cool. Serve warm or cold. To store, place cooled pie uncovered in refrigerator or place in an airtight container and freeze.

Yield: One 9-inch pie (8 servings)

PER SERVING (FILLING ONLY)

Calories: 122.4
Protein: 0.9 g
Fat: 3.4 g
Carbohydrate: 21.1 g

Sodium: 1.1 mg
Diabetic exchanges
  Fat: 1
  Fruit: 1½

Cherry-Prune Pie

Two 16-ounce packages frozen dark
   sweet cherries, thawed and
   drained
8 pitted prunes (medium)
2 tablespoons vegetable oil
2 tablespoons unsweetened apple juice
   concentrate (any brand)

1 tablespoon water
¼ teaspoon lemon juice
1½ to 2 tablespoons Minute tapioca
One 9-inch pie shell of choice (see
   pages 85–95) plus top crust or
   topping of choice (see pages
   122–134)

1. Preheat oven to 450°F.
2. Puree 12 of the cherries, the prunes, oil, concentrate, and water in a blender.
3. In a large bowl, stir together fruit puree, remaining cherries, lemon juice, and tapioca; allow mixture to sit for 10 minutes. Pour mixture into pie shell of choice and add topping or crust of choice.
4. Bake at 450°F for 15 minutes. Reduce oven to 350°F and continue baking for 35 minutes, or until topping or crust is golden.
5. Remove pie plate from oven and place on a wire rack to cool. Serve warm or cold. To store, place cooled pie uncovered in refrigerator or place in an airtight container and freeze.

Yield: One 9-inch pie (8 servings)

PER SERVING (FILLING ONLY)

Calories: 137.9
Protein: 1.1 g
Fat: 3.5 g
Carbohydrate: 25.2 g

Sodium: 1.4 mg
Diabetic exchanges
  Fat: ½
  Fruit: 2

Mixed Granola Pie

2 cups peeled, pitted, and sliced
   peaches
1 pear, peeled, cored, and diced
1 cup frozen blueberries, thawed and
   drained
½ cup frozen red raspberries, thawed
   and drained
½ cup frozen black raspberries, thawed
   and drained
2 plums, peeled, pitted, and diced

4 tablespoons Minute tapioca
1 tablespoon vegetable oil
½ teaspoon lemon juice
½ teaspoon cinnamon
One 10-inch Mixed Granola Pie Crust
   (page 94) or pie shell of choice (see
   pages 85–95) plus top crust or
   topping of choice (see pages
   122–134)

1. Preheat oven to 350°F.

2. In a large bowl, stir together all ingredients and allow mixture to sit for 10 minutes.

3. Pour mixture into Mixed Granola Pie Crust. Sprinkle granola topping over filling or use crust or topping of choice.

4. Bake 55 minutes, or until crust or topping is golden.

5. Remove pie from oven and place on a wire rack to cool. Serve warm or cold. To store, place cooled pie uncovered in refrigerator or place in an airtight container and freeze.

Yield: One 10-inch pie (8 servings)

PER SERVING (FILLING ONLY)

Calories: 85	*Sodium:* 1.6 mg
Protein: 0.7 g	*Diabetic exchanges*
Fat: 2.1 g	*Fat:* ½
Carbohydrate: 17.4 g	*Fruit:* 1

Peach Pie

4 cups peeled, pitted, and sliced
   peaches
½ teaspoon cinnamon
4 to 4½ tablespoons Minute tapioca
2 tablespoons vegetable shortening,
   vegetable oil, or lard

½ to ¾ cup unsweetened apple juice
   concentrate (any brand)
One 9-inch pie shell of choice (see
   pages 85–95) plus top crust or
   topping of choice (see pages
   122–134)

1. Preheat oven to 350°F.

2. In a large bowl, stir together peaches, cinnamon, tapioca, shortening, and concentrate; allow mixture to sit for 10 minutes. Pour mixture into pie shell of choice and add topping or crust of choice.

3. Bake 55 minutes, or until topping or crust is golden.

4. Remove pie from oven and place on a wire rack to cool. Serve warm or cold. To store, place cooled pie uncovered in refrigerator or place in an airtight container and freeze.

Yield: One 9-inch pie (8 servings)

PER SERVING (FILLING ONLY)

Calories: 114
Protein: 0.7 g
Fat: 3.4 g
Carbohydrate: 21.8 g

Sodium: 4.4 mg
Diabetic exchanges
  Fat: ½
  Fruit: 1½

Peach-Prune Pie

10 pitted prunes (medium)
½ cup plus 2 tablespoons water
2 tablespoons vegetable oil
4 cups peaches, peeled, pitted, and
 sliced

½ teaspoon cinnamon
¼ cup Minute tapioca
One 9-inch pie shell of choice (see pages
 85–95) plus top crust or topping of
 choice (see pages 122–134)

1. Preheat oven to 350°F.

2. Puree prunes, water, and oil in a blender.

3. In a large bowl, stir together puree, peaches, cinnamon, and tapioca; allow mixture to sit for 5 minutes. Pour mixture into pie shell of choice and add topping or crust of choice.

4. Bake 50 to 55 minutes, or until topping or crust is golden.

5. Remove pie from oven and place on a wire rack to cool. Serve warm or cold. To store, place cooled pie uncovered in refrigerator or place in an airtight container and freeze.

Yield: One 9-inch pie (8 servings)

PER SERVING (FILLING ONLY)

Calories: 112
Protein: 0.9 g
Fat: 3.5 g
Carbohydrate: 21.2 g

Sodium: 0.5 mg
Diabetic exchanges
 Fat: 1
 Fruit: 1½

Raspberry-Peach Pie

¾ to 1 cup fresh or frozen, thawed, and
   drained red raspberries
2 tablespoons water
3 to 4 peaches, peeled, pitted, and sliced
¼ to ⅓ cup unsweetened apple juice
   concentrate (any brand)
3 tablespoons Minute tapioca

1 tablespoon vegetable shortening,
   vegetable oil, or lard
2 tablespoons *dry* coconut (optional)
One 9-inch pie shell of choice (see pages
   85–95) plus top crust or topping of
   choice (see pages 122–134)

1. Preheat oven to 350°F.

2. Puree raspberries and water in a blender. Strain puree through a small hand strainer, discarding seeds.

3. In a large bowl, stir together puree, peaches, concentrate, tapioca, shortening, and coconut; allow mixture to sit for 5 minutes. Pour mixture into pie shell of choice and add topping or crust of choice.

4. Bake 55 minutes, or until topping or crust is golden.

5. Remove pie from oven and place on a wire rack to cool. Serve warm or cold. To store, place cooled pie uncovered in refrigerator or place in an airtight container and freeze.

Yield: One 9-inch pie (8 servings)

PER SERVING (FILLING ONLY)

Calories: 63
Protein: 0.4 g
Fat: 1.7 g
Carbohydrate: 12.3 g

Sodium: 2.2 mg
Diabetic exchanges
  Fruit: 1
  Fat: ½

Rhubarb-Apple Pie

1 cup plus 2 tablespoons (9 ounces)
   unsweetened apple juice
   concentrate (any brand)
6 tablespoons Minute tapioca
2 tablespoons vegetable shortening,
   vegetable oil, or lard

1 quart chopped rhubarb
One 9-inch pie shell of choice (see pages
   85–95) plus top crust or topping (see
   pages 122–134)

1. Preheat oven to 350°F.

2. In a large bowl, stir together concentrate, tapioca, shortening, and rhubarb; allow mixture to sit for 10 minutes.

3. Pour mixture into pie shell of choice. Top with crust or topping of choice.

4. Bake 60 to 65 minutes, or until crust or topping is golden.

5. Remove pie plate from oven and place on a wire rack to cool. Serve warm or cold. To store, place cooled pie uncovered in refrigerator, or place in an airtight container and freeze.

Yield: One 9-inch pie (8 servings)

PER SERVING (FILLING ONLY)

Calories: 124
Protein: 0.7 g
Fat: 3.4 g
Carbohydrate: 23.3 g

Sodium: 10.4 mg
Diabetic exchanges
Fat: ½
Fruit: 1½

Rhubarb-Strawberry-Apple Pie

1 cup plus 2 tablespoons (9 ounces)
  unsweetened apple juice
  concentrate (any brand)
6 tablespoons Minute tapioca
2 tablespoons vegetable shortening or
  vegetable oil

2 cups chopped rhubarb
2½ cups sliced fresh strawberries
One 9-inch pie shell of choice (see pages
  85–95) plus top crust or topping
  (see pages 122–134)

1. Preheat oven to 350°F.

2. In a large bowl, stir together concentrate, tapioca, shortening, rhubarb, and fresh strawberries; allow mixture to sit for 10 minutes.

3. Pour mixture into pie shell of choice. Top with crust or topping of choice.

4. Bake 55 minutes, or until crust or topping is golden.

5. Remove pie plate from oven and place on a wire rack to cool. Serve warm or cold. To store, place cooled pie uncovered in refrigerator, or place in an airtight container and freeze.

Yield: One 9-inch pie (8 servings)

PER SERVING (FILLING ONLY)

Calories: 133
Protein: 0.8 g
Fat: 3.6 g
Carbohydrate: 25.6 g
Sodium: 9.7 mg

Diabetic exchanges
Starch: 1
Fat: ½
Fruit: 1

Pecan Pie

6 egg whites or 3 extralarge eggs
½ teaspoon salt
¾ cup brown-rice syrup (Sweet
 Dreams Brown Rice Syrup by
 Lundberg or Westbrae Natural
 Brown Rice Syrup)
Scant 3 tablespoons unsweetened apple
 juice concentrate (any brand)

¼ cup plus 1 tablespoon vegetable
 shortening, melted and slightly
 cooled
1¼ cups pecan halves
One 9-inch pie shell of choice (see pages
 85–95) (see *Note*)

1. Preheat oven to 325°F.

2. Beat eggs using a hand-operated mechanical beater. Add salt and brown-rice syrup; stir. Add concentrate, and then shortening, stirring well after each addition. Stir in pecans. Pour filling into prepared pie shell.

3. Bake 48 minutes or until a knife inserted into center of pie comes out mostly clean. Do not overbake or you may burn the pecans. Serve warm or cold. To store, place cooled pie, uncovered, in refrigerator.

Yield: One 9-inch pie (8 servings)

PER SERVING (FILLING ONLY)

Calories: 267
Protein: 4.0 g
Fat: 19.4 g
Carbohydrate: 21.0 g

Sodium: 178 mg
Diabetic exchanges
 Starch: 1½
 Fat: 4

Note: To make this pie gluten-free, make sure label on brown-rice syrup states "gluten-free," and use either Prebaked Brown Rice Pie Crust (pages 92 or 93) for pie shell. Remember to prebake the crust for only 10 minutes, then pour filling into shell and bake according to directions.

Pumpkin Pie

4 egg whites or 2 extralarge eggs
One 15-ounce can solid-pack pumpkin
   (Libby's 100% Natural)
½ cup brown-rice syrup (Sweet
   Dreams Brown Rice Syrup by
   Lundberg or Westbrae Natural
   Brown Rice Syrup)
½ teaspoon salt

1¾ teaspoons cinnamon
Generous ¾ teaspoon ginger
Scant ½ teaspoon cloves
¼ cup unsweetened apple juice
   concentrate (any brand)
¼ cup plus 2 tablespoons water
One 9-inch pie shell of choice (see pages
   85–95) (see *Note*)

1. Preheat oven to 400°F.

2. In a large bowl, beat eggs lightly with a fork. Add pumpkin, brown-rice syrup, salt, cinnamon, ginger, cloves, concentrate, and water, stirring after each addition. Pour filling into prepared pie shell.

3. Bake 15 minutes, turn oven down to 350°F, and bake pie for another 42 to 43 minutes, or until a knife inserted into the center of pie comes out clean.

4. Remove pie from oven and place on a wire rack to cool. Serve warm or cold. To store, place cooled pie, uncovered, in refrigerator.

Yield: One 9-inch pie (8 servings)

PER SERVING (FILLING ONLY)

Calories: 83
Protein: 2.4 g
Fat: 0.2 g
Carbohydrate: 18.7 g

Sodium: 168 mg
Diabetic exchanges
   Starch: ½
   Fruit: 1

Note: To make this pie gluten-free, make sure label on brown-rice syrup states "gluten-free," and use either Prebaked Brown Rice Pie Crust (page 92 or 93) for pie shell. Remember to prebake the crust for only 10 minutes, then pour filling into shell and bake according to directions.

FRUIT
CRISPS
AND
TOPPINGS

Fruit crisps make wonderful desserts. They call for fresh natural produce (but you may substitute frozen fruit if fresh is not available), they are simple and quick to prepare (no crust necessary, as with pies), and they can be served warm right from the baking dish. Here are just a few hints for making your crisps "crispy" and delicious:

- Make sure you drain the fruit well.
- You may use a bit more or less of each fruit concentrate, depending on desired sweetness. Just remember that if you use more concentrate than called for in a recipe, you may need to add more tapioca as the thickener.
- When a recipe calls for *dry* coconut, do not premoisten it; the coconut will get its moisture from the fruit.
- Too much shortening or lard in a topping will make it too wet; not enough will make it too dry. As this is very much a matter of taste, you may need to experiment with the lard/shortening quantities in the toppings until you get the desired result.
- A topping made of just flour, shortening, and cinnamon does not work well. You need to add coconut or seeds or chopped nuts or rolled oats (or all these things) to make a good topping. Feel free to experiment with the recipes in this chapter and create your own unique topping.
- When lard or shortening is used in the fruit filling, be sure to melt it before mixing it with the fruit; otherwise, you may get a wet spot under the topping.
- Whenever possible, bake your crisps in glass or ceramic baking dishes rather than in metal baking pans. A glass dish makes a more attractive serving dish, and, even if you refrigerate the crisp for a day or two, a glass dish won't become stained; nor will there be a chemical reaction with the acid from the fruit.

Fruit-Berry Crisp

2 cups peeled, pitted, and diced peaches
¾ cup fresh or frozen, thawed, and
    drained red raspberries
¾ cup fresh or frozen, thawed, and
    drained blueberries

Scant ½ teaspoon cinnamon
4 tablespoons Minute tapioca
Crispy Oat Topping (see page 129) or
    topping of choice

1. Preheat oven to 350°F. Oil a 9- by 9- by 2-inch glass or ceramic baking dish.

2. In a large bowl, stir together all ingredients except topping. Spread fruit in prepared dish. Let sit 10 minutes. Add topping.

3. Bake 50 to 55 minutes, or until topping is crisp looking and slightly golden.

4. Remove dish from oven and place on a wire rack to cool. Serve warm or cold. Store uncovered cooled crisp in refrigerator. Freeze in portions.

Yield: 9 servings

PER SERVING (WITHOUT TOPPING)

Calories: 42
Protein: 0.4 g
Fat: 0.2 g
Carbohydrate: 10.4 g

Sodium: 1.0 mg
Diabetic exchanges
    Fruit: ⅔

Holiday Crisp

2 cups peeled, cored, and diced apples

1 cup peeled, cored, and diced pears or peaches

Generous ½ cup fresh or frozen, blueberries (thawed and drained if frozen)

10 dark, sweet, seedless cherries

3 to 3½ tablespoons Minute tapioca

Scant ½ teaspoon cinnamon

1 tablespoon vegetable oil

⅓ to ½ cup unsweetened apple juice concentrate (any brand)

Pecan Topping (see page 131) or Quick Brown Rice-Seed Topping (see page 123) or topping of choice

1. Preheat oven to 350°F. Oil a 9- by 9- by 2-inch glass or ceramic baking dish.

2. In a large bowl, stir together all ingredients except topping. Pour mixture into prepared dish and add topping.

3. Bake 50 to 55 minutes, or until topping is crisp looking and slightly golden.

4. Remove dish from oven and place on a wire rack to cool. Serve warm or cold. Store uncovered cooled crisp in refrigerator. Freeze in portions.

Yield: 9 servings

PER SERVING (WITHOUT TOPPING)

Calories: 79

Protein: 0.3 g

Fat: 1.8 g

Carbohydrate: 16.4 g

Sodium: 3.1 mg

Diabetic exchanges

  Fat: ½

  Fruit: 1

Mixed Fruit Crisp

1 large or 2 small pears, peeled, cored, and sliced

2 peaches, peeled, pitted, and sliced (1 cup)

1 large or 2 small nectarines, peeled and sliced (1 cup)

2 large or 3 small plums, diced

10 dark, sweet, seedless cherries

Generous ½ cup fresh or frozen, thawed, and drained red raspberries

Generous ½ cup fresh or frozen, thawed, and drained black raspberries

Generous ½ cup fresh or frozen, thawed, and drained blueberries

⅓ cup chopped rhubarb

5 tablespoons Minute tapioca

¼ teaspoon cinnamon

1 tablespoon vegetable shortening (melted), vegetable oil, or lard (melted)

Sesame Topping (see page 132) or topping of choice

1. Preheat oven to 350°F. Oil a 13- by 9- by 2-inch glass or ceramic baking dish.

2. In a large bowl, stir together all fruit and rhubarb. Add tapioca, cinnamon, and shortening; stir well. Spread fruit in prepared dish and add topping.

3. Bake 55 to 60 minutes, or until topping is crisp looking and slightly golden.

4. Remove dish from oven and place on a wire rack to cool. Serve warm or cold. Store uncovered cooled crisp in refrigerator. Freeze in portions.

Yield: 15 servings

PER SERVING (WITHOUT TOPPING)

Calories: 53	*Sodium:* 0.3 mg
Protein: 0.6 g	*Diabetic exchanges*
Fat: 1.1 g	*Fat:* ¼
Carbohydrate: 11.5 g	*Fruit:* ¾

Apple or Pear Crisp

4 cups peeled, cored, and diced apple or
    pear
½ teaspoon cinnamon
2½ tablespoons Minute tapioca
2 tablespoons vegetable oil

½ cup unsweetened apple juice
    concentrate (any brand)
Pecan Topping (see page 131), Whole-
    Wheat 'n' Walnut Topping (see
    page 134), or topping of choice

1. Preheat oven to 350°F. Oil a 9- by 9- by 2-inch glass or ceramic baking dish.

2. In a large bowl, stir together all ingredients except topping. Pour mixture into prepared dish and add topping.

3. Bake 50 to 55 minutes, or until topping is crisp looking and slightly golden.

4. Remove dish from oven and place on a wire rack to cool. Serve warm or cold. Store uncovered cooled crisp in refrigerator. Freeze in portions.

Yield: 9 servings

PER SERVING (WITHOUT TOPPING)

Calories: 92
Protein: 0.2 g
Fat: 3.2 g
Carbohydrate: 16.5 g

Sodium: 3.9 mg
Diabetic exchanges
  Fat: ½
  Fruit: 1

Blueberry Crisp

¾ cup fresh blueberries

3 tablespoons water

2 cups fresh or frozen, thawed, and
   drained blueberries

3 tablespoons Minute tapioca

1 tablespoon vegetable oil

Barley Topping (see page 122) or
   topping of choice

1. Preheat oven to 350°F. Oil a 9- by 9- by 2-inch glass or ceramic baking dish.

2. Puree ¾ cup blueberries and water in a blender.

3. In a large bowl, stir together blueberry puree and remaining blueberries. Stir in tapioca and oil. Pour mixture into prepared baking dish and let sit for 10 minutes. Add topping.

4. Bake 50 minutes, or until topping is crisp looking and slightly golden.

5. Remove dish from oven and place on a wire rack to cool. Serve warm or cold. Store uncovered cooled crisp in refrigerator. Freeze in portions.

Yield: 9 servings

PER SERVING (WITHOUT TOPPING)

Calories: 51

Protein: 0.3 g

Fat: 1.9 g

Carbohydrate: 9.3 g

Sodium: 2.7 mg

Diabetic exchanges

  Fat: ⅓

  Fruit: ⅔

Cherry Crisp

2 cups fresh or frozen, thawed, and
   drained dark sweet cherries
2 tablespoons vegetable oil
3 tablespoons plus 1½ teaspoons
   Minute tapioca

⅓ to ½ cup unsweetened apple juice
   concentrate (any brand)
2 tablespoons water
Double-Oat Topping (see page 130) or
   topping of choice

1. Preheat oven to 350°F. Oil a 9- by 9- by 2-inch glass or ceramic baking dish.

2. In a large bowl, stir together all ingredients except topping. Pour mixture into prepared baking dish and let sit for 10 minutes. Add topping.

3. Bake 50 minutes, or until topping is crisp looking and slightly golden.

4. Remove dish from oven and place on a wire rack to cool. Serve warm or cold. Store uncovered cooled crisp in refrigerator. Freeze in portions.

Yield: 9 servings

PER SERVING (WITHOUT TOPPING)

Calories: 83
Protein: 0.4 g
Fat: 3.4 g
Carbohydrate: 13.5 g

Sodium: 2.6 mg
Diabetic exchanges
  Fat: ½
  Fruit: 1

Peach Crisp

4 cups peeled, pitted, and thinly sliced
  peaches
5 tablespoons Minute tapioca
2 tablespoons vegetable shortening
  (melted), vegetable oil, or lard
  (melted)

½ cup unsweetened apple juice
  concentrate (any brand)
½ teaspoon cinnamon
Pecan Topping (see page 131) or
  topping of choice

1. Preheat oven to 350°F. Oil a 9- by 9- by 2-inch glass or ceramic baking dish.

2. Drain peaches well and pat dry with a paper towel.

3. In a large bowl, stir together all ingredients except topping. Pour into prepared baking dish and let sit for 10 minutes. Add topping.

4. Bake 55 minutes, or until topping is crisp looking and slightly golden.

5. Remove dish from oven and place on a wire rack to cool. Serve warm or cold. Store uncovered cooled crisp in refrigerator. Freeze in portions.

Yield: 9 servings

PER SERVING (WITHOUT TOPPING)

Calories: 106
Protein: 0.6 g
Fat: 3.0 g
Carbohydrate: 20.5 g

Sodium: 3.9 mg
Diabetic exchanges
Fat: ½
Fruit: 1½

Peaches 'n' Berries Crisp

⅓ cup fresh or frozen, thawed, and
drained red raspberries
⅓ cup fresh or frozen, thawed, and
drained black raspberries
4 tablespoons water
3½ cups peeled, pitted, and sliced
peaches

1 tablespoon vegetable oil
½ teaspoon cinnamon
Generous 5 tablespoons Minute tapioca
Wheat Germ Topping (see page 133) or
topping of choice

1. Preheat oven to 350°F. Oil a 9- by 9- by 2-inch glass or ceramic baking dish.
2. Puree red and black raspberries and water in a blender. Press puree through a strainer and discard seeds.
3. In a large bowl, stir together raspberry puree, peaches, oil, cinnamon, and tapioca. Pour mixture into prepared dish and add topping.
4. Bake 50 to 55 minutes, or until topping is crisp looking and slightly golden.
5. Remove dish from oven and place on a wire rack to cool. Serve warm or cold. Store uncovered cooled crisp in refrigerator. Freeze in portions.

Yield: 9 servings

PER SERVING (WITHOUT TOPPING)

Calories: 62
Protein: 0.5 g
Fat: 1.6 g
Carbohydrate: 11.9 g

Sodium: 0.4 mg
Diabetic exchanges
  Fat: ¼
  Fruit: ¾

Pear Crisp

4 cups peeled, cored, and diced pears
   (set aside ¼ cup)
1¼ cups peeled, pitted, and sliced
   peaches
½ teaspoon cinnamon
3 tablespoons plus 1½ teaspoons
   Minute tapioca
2 tablespoons vegetable shortening
   (melted), vegetable oil, or lard
   (melted)

2 tablespoons *dry*, unsweetened
   coconut *or* 1 tablespoon poppy or
   sesame seeds *or* 2 tablespoons
   chopped nuts
Nutty Nutmeg Topping (see page 128),
   Barley-Cashew Topping (see page
   125), or topping of choice

1. Preheat oven to 350°F. Oil a 9- by 9- by 2-inch glass or ceramic baking dish.

2. Puree ¼ cup pears and the peaches in a blender.

3. In a large bowl, stir together remaining 3¾ cups diced pears, pureed fruit, cinnamon, tapioca, shortening, and coconut (or seeds or nuts). Pour mixture into prepared dish and let sit for 10 minutes. Add topping.

4. Bake 55 minutes, or until topping is crisp looking and slightly golden.

5. Remove dish from oven and place on a wire rack to cool. Serve warm or cold. Store uncovered cooled crisp in refrigerator. Freeze in portions.

Yield: 9 servings

PER SERVING (WITHOUT TOPPING)

Calories: 83
Protein: 0.5 g
Fat: 3.3 g
Carbohydrate: 14.2 g

Sodium: 0.8 mg
Diabetic exchanges
   Fat: ½
   Fruit: 1

Pineapple Crisp

One 20-ounce can unsweetened pineapple rings (use Dole if you are allergic to phenol)

2 cups peeled and diced nectarines

1/2 cup peeled, pitted, and diced plums, patted dry

1/3 cup unsweetened apple juice concentrate (any brand)

4 tablespoons Minute tapioca

1/2 teaspoon cinnamon

Nut and Seed Topping (see page 129) or topping of choice

1. Preheat oven to 350°F. Oil a 9- by 9- by 2-inch glass or ceramic baking dish.

2. Drain pineapple slices and pat dry. Chop into bite-sized pieces.

3. In a large bowl, stir together all ingredients except topping. Pour mixture into prepared baking dish and add topping.

4. Bake 50 to 55 minutes, or until topping is crisp looking and slightly golden.

5. Remove baking dish from oven and place on a wire rack to cool. Serve warm or cold. Store uncovered cooled crisp in refrigerator. Freeze in portions.

Yield: 9 servings

PER SERVING (WITHOUT TOPPING)

Calories: 93
Protein: 0.7 g
Fat: 0.3 g
Carbohydrate: 23.5 g

Sodium: 3.2 mg
Diabetic exchanges
   Fruit: 1 1/2

Pineapple-Rhubarb Crisp

3 cups chopped rhubarb
1 tablespoon vegetable oil
⅓ cup plus 1 tablespoon Minute
  tapioca
1½ cups unsweetened apple juice
  concentrate (any brand)
One 20-ounce can unsweetened
  pineapple rings (use Dole if you are
  allergic to phenol), cut up and
  drained

¼ cup *dry* unsweetened coconut
  (optional)
Whole-Wheat and Sesame Topping
  (see page 134) or topping of choice

1. Preheat oven to 350°F. Oil a 10- by 8- by 2-inch glass or ceramic baking dish.

2. In a large bowl, stir together all ingredients except topping. Pour mixture into prepared baking dish and let sit for 10 minutes. Add topping.

3. Bake 60 to 65 minutes, or until topping is crisp looking and slightly golden.

4. Remove dish from oven and place on a wire rack to cool. Serve warm or cold. Store uncovered cooled crisp in refrigerator. Freeze in portions.

Yield: 9 servings

PER SERVING (WITHOUT TOPPING)

Calories: 165
Protein: 0.9 g
Fat: 1.8 g
Carbohydrate: 38.0 g
Sodium: 14.0 mg

Diabetic exchanges
Starch: ½
Fat: ½
Fruit: 2

Barley Topping

¾ cup pearled barley (see *Note*)
3 tablespoons barley flour
1 tablespoon sesame seeds
2 tablespoons vegetable oil
1 tablespoon water
Optional: ¼ cup unsweetened coconut,
   premoistened with 1 teaspoon
   water and 1 teaspoon vegetable oil;
   or ¼ cup seeds; *or* ¼ cup chopped
   nuts; *or* ¼ cup rolled oats; *or* any
   combination of the above

1. In a medium-sized bowl, stir together all ingredients.
2. Spoon on top of any pie or fruit mixture.

Yield: Enough topping for one crisp or one 9-inch pie (8.5 servings)

PER SERVING

Calories: 103   *Sodium:* 0.9 mg
Protein: 1.9 g   *Diabetic exchanges*
Fat: 3.9 g   *Starch:* 1
Carbohydrate: 15.7 g   *Fat:* ¾

Note: You can grind a portion of the pearled barley in your blender for a few seconds to make it more fine if you wish.

Prebaked Rice Crumb-Crust Topping

Gluten-Free

1 Prebaked Brown Rice Pie Crust,
  either using shortening (page 000) or
  oil (page 000)

½ to ¾ cup toasted chopped pecans or
  toasted nuts of choice
½ teaspoon cinnamon

1. In a large bowl, and using your hands, crush Prebaked Brown Rice Pie Crust. Add toasted chopped nuts and cinnamon. Mix ingredients well using a large spoon.

2. Spoon half of topping over any precooked pie filling or fruit mixture. Extra topping can be placed in a plastic bag and frozen for later use.

Yield: Enough topping for two 9-inch pies or two crisps (17 servings)

PER SERVING

Calories: 23.5
Protein: 0.3 g
Fat: 2.4 g
Carbohydrate: 0.7 g

Sodium: 0.1 mg
Diabetic exchanges
  Fat: ½

Quick Brown Rice-Seed Topping

Gluten-Free

¾ cup plus 2 tablespoons brown rice
  flour
1 tablespoon plus 2 teaspoons poppy
  seeds
1 tablespoon plus 2 teaspoons sesame
  seeds

¼ cup chopped pecans
¼ teaspoon cinnamon
3 tablespoons vegetable oil

1. In a medium-sized bowl, mix all ingredients with a fork.

2. Spoon topping over any fruit crisp or pie filling and smooth topping lightly with spoon.

Yield: Enough topping for one crisp or one 9-inch pie (8.5 servings)

PER SERVING

Calories: 135   *Sodium:* 0.6 mg
Protein: 2.1 g   *Diabetic exchanges*
Fat: 9.2 g   *Starch:* 1
Carbohydrate: 12.6 g   *Fat:* 2

Spelt 'N' Nut Topping

Has Gluten

¾ cup spelt flour   Generous ¼ teaspoon cinnamon
½ cup chopped pecans   3 tablespoons vegetable oil

1. In a medium-sized bowl, mix all ingredients with a fork.
2. Sprinkle topping over any pie or fruit mixture.

Yield: Enough topping for one crisp or one 9-inch pie (8.5 servings)

PER SERVING

Calories: 128   *Sodium:* 0.1 mg
Protein: 2.3 g   *Diabetic exchanges*
Fat: 9.9 g   *Starch:* ½
Carbohydrate: 9.5 g   *Fat:* 2

Barley-Cashew Topping

¾ cup pearled barley (see *Note*)
¼ cup chopped cashews
3 tablespoons barley flour

¼ teaspoon cinnamon
2 tablespoons vegetable oil

1. In a medium-sized bowl, stir together all ingredients.
2. Spoon topping over any pie or fruit mixture and smooth topping by hand.

Yield: Enough topping for one crisp or one 9-inch pie (8.5 servings)

PER SERVING

Calories: 119
Protein: 2.3 g
Fat: 5.0 g
Carbohydrate: 16.8 g

Sodium: 0.5 mg
Diabetic exchanges
   Starch: 1
   Fat: 1

Note: You can grind a portion of the pearled barley in your blender for a few seconds to make it more fine if you wish.

Barley-Rice Topping

¼ to ⅓ cup pearled barley
3 tablespoons white-rice flour
3 tablespoons barley flour
½ cup chopped nuts

¼ to ½ teaspoon cinnamon
Generous 1 tablespoon vegetable
   shortening or lard

1. In a medium-sized bowl, stir together all ingredients with a fork.
2. Spoon topping over any pie or fruit mixture and smooth topping by hand gently.

Yield: Enough topping for one 9-inch pie or one crisp (8.5 servings)

PER SERVING (IF USING PECANS FOR CHOPPED NUTS)

Calories: 91   *Sodium:* 0.3 mg
Protein: 1.4 g   *Diabetic exchanges*
Fat: 6.3 g   *Starch:* ½
Carbohydrate: 8.7 g   *Fat:* 1¼

Teff-Nut Topping

Has Gluten

½ cup plus 1 to 2 tablespoons teff flour   ¼ cup chopped walnuts

¼ to ½ teaspoon cinnamon   Scant 2 tablespoons water

2 tablespoons sesame seeds   2 tablespoons vegetable oil

1. In a medium-sized bowl, stir together all ingredients with a fork, working ingredients together well.

2. Sprinkle topping on top of any pie or fruit mixture.

Yield: Enough topping for one crisp or one 9-inch pie (8.5 servings)

PER SERVING

Calories: 100   *Sodium:* 1.9 mg
Protein: 2.2 g   *Diabetic exchages*
Fat: 6.7 g   *Starch:* ½
Carbohydrate: 8.9 g   *Fat:* 1

Amaranth Topping

Gluten-Free

½ cup amaranth flour
¼ teaspoon cinnamon
¼ cup chopped nuts
2 tablespoons to 2 tablespoons plus ¼
   teaspoon vegetable oil

Optional: ¼ cup unsweetened coconut,
   premoistened with 1 teaspoon
   water and 1 teaspoon vegetable oil,
   or ¼ cup seeds

1. In a medium-sized bowl, mix all ingredients with a fork.
2. Spoon topping over any pie or fruit mixture and smooth topping by hand.

Yield: Enough topping for one crisp or one 9-inch pie (8.5 servings)

PER SERVING (IF USING PECANS FOR CHOPPED NUTS)

Calories: 78
Protein: 1.2 g
Fat: 5.9 g
Carbohydrate: 5.2 g

Sodium: 0.5 mg
Diabetic exchanges
  Starch: ½
  Fat: 1

Nutty Nutmeg Topping

¾ cup all-purpose flour
⅓ cup chopped nuts of choice
1½ tablespoons unsweetened coconut,
   premoistened with ½ teaspoon
   water and ½ teaspoon vegetable oil
   (optional)

1½ teaspoons sesame seeds
4 tablespoons vegetable shortening or
   lard
¼ teaspoon cinnamon
⅛ teaspoon nutmeg

1. In a medium-sized bowl, mix all ingredients with a fork.
2. Spoon topping over any pie or fruit mixture and smooth topping by hand.

Yield: Enough topping for one crisp or one 9-inch pie (8.5 servings)

PER SERVING (USING PECANS FOR CHOPPED NUTS)

Calories: 126
Protein: 1.6 g
Fat: 9.6 g
Carbohydrate: 9.8 g
Sodium: 0.4 mg

Diabetic exchanges
  Starch: ½
  Fat: 2

Nut and Seed Topping

½ cup chopped nuts of choice
1 tablespoon poppy seeds
1 tablespoon sesame seeds

1 tablespoon sunflower seeds
¼ teaspoon cinnamon

1. In a medium-sized bowl, mix all ingredients with a fork.
2. Spoon topping over any pie or fruit mixture and smooth topping by hand.

Yield: Enough topping for one crisp or one 9-inch pie (8.5 servings)

PER SERVING

Calories: 64
Protein: 1.1 g
Fat: 6.2 g
Carbohydrate: 2.1 g

Sodium: 0.5 mg
Diabetic exchanges
  Fat: 1

Crispy Oat Topping

⅓ cup all-purpose flour
½ cup rolled oats
Optional: ⅓ cup unsweetened coconut,
  premoistened with 1½ teaspoons
  water and 1½ teaspoons vegetable

oil; *or* ⅓ cup raw, hulled sunflower
  seeds; *or* ⅓ cup chopped nuts
4 tablespoons vegetable shortening or
  lard
¼ teaspoon cinnamon

1. In a medium-sized bowl, mix all ingredients with a fork.
2. Spoon topping over any pie or fruit mixture and smooth topping by hand.

Yield: Enough topping for one crisp or one 9-inch pie (8.5 servings)

PER SERVING

Calories: 87
Protein: 1.4 g
Fat: 6.1 g
Carbohydrate: 7.3 g

Sodium: 0.1 mg
Diabetic exchanges
  Starch: ½
  Fat: 1

Coconut-Nut Topping

½ cup unsweetened coconut, premoistened with 3 teaspoons water and 3 teaspoons vegetable oil

⅓ cup chopped walnuts
¼ teaspoon cinnamon

1. In a medium-sized bowl, stir together all ingredients with a fork.
2. Sprinkle topping over any pie or fruit mixture and smooth topping by hand.

Yield: Enough topping for one crisp or one 9-inch pie (8.5 servings)

PER SERVING

Calories: 74
Protein: 1.5 g
Fat: 7.3 g
Carbohydrate: 1.8 g

Sodium: 1.8 mg
Diabetic exchanges
Fat: 1½

Double-Oat Topping

½ to ¾ cup rolled oats
¼ cup oat flour
3 tablespoons vegetable oil
2 tablespoons sesame seeds
⅛ to ¼ teaspoon cinnamon

Optional: ¼ cup unsweetened coconut, premoistened with 1 teaspoon water and 1 teaspoon vegetable oil; *or* ¼ cup seeds and ¼ cup chopped nuts

1. In a medium-sized bowl, stir together all ingredients with a fork.
2. Spoon topping over any pie or fruit mixture and smooth topping by hand.

Yield: Enough topping for one crisp or one 9-inch pie (8.5 servings)

PER SERVING

Calories: 83
Protein: 1.9 g
Fat: 6.3 g
Carbohydrate: 5.5 g

Sodium: 0.8 mg
Diabetic exchanges
Starch: ⅓
Fat: 1¼

Pecan Topping

¾ cup all-purpose flour
⅓ cup chopped pecans
Generous ¼ teaspoon cinnamon
¼ cup vegetable shortening or lard

1. In a medium-sized bowl, stir together all ingredients.
2. Spoon topping over any pie or fruit mixture and smooth topping by hand.

Yield: Enough topping for one crisp or one 9-inch pie (8.5 servings)

PER SERVING

Calories: 123
Protein: 1.5 g
Fat: 9.1 g
Carbohydrate: 9.2 g

Sodium: 0.3 mg
Diabetic exchanges
  Starch: ½
  Fat: 2

Sesame Topping

¾ to 1 cup all-purpose flour
1½ tablespoons sesame seeds
Optional: ⅓ cup unsweetened coconut,
   premoistened with 1½ teaspoons
   water and 1½ teaspoons vegetable
   oil plus 1 teaspoon poppy seeds; *or* ¼
   cup chopped nuts; *or* ¼ cup rolled
   oats; *or* any combination of above

¼ cup plus 1½ to 2 tablespoons
   vegetable shortening or lard
Generous ¼ teaspoon cinnamon

1. In a medium-sized bowl, mix all ingredients with a fork.
2. Spoon topping over any pie or fruit mixture and smooth topping by hand.

Yield: Enough for one 13- by 9- by 2-inch crisp (15 servings)

PER SERVING

Calories: 69
Protein: 0.8 g
Fat: 5.1 g
Carbohydrate: 4.9 g

Sodium: 0.4 mg
Diabetic exchanges
  Starch: ⅓
  Fat: 1

Roasted Sunflower Topping

⅓ cup roasted sunflower seeds

⅛ teaspoon cinnamon

1. In a small bowl, stir together sunflower seeds and cinnamon.
2. Sprinkle topping over any pie or fruit mixture.

Yield: Enough topping for one crisp or one 9-inch pie (8.5 servings)

PER SERVING

Calories: 34
Protein: 1.1 g
Fat: 2.9 g
Carbohydrate: 1.4 g

Sodium: 0
Diabetic exchange
  Fat: ¾

Super-Energy Topping

¾ cup rolled oats
⅓ cup oat flour
¼ cup chopped almonds or other nut
   of choice

2 tablespoons sesame seeds
1 teaspoon poppy seeds
3 tablespoons vegetable oil

1. In a medium-sized bowl, stir together all ingredients.
2. Spoon topping over any pie or fruit mixture and smooth topping by hand.

Yield: Enough topping for one crisp or one 9-inch pie (8.5 servings)

PER SERVING

Calories: 121
Protein: 3.3 g
Fat: 8.9 g
Carbohydrate: 8.8 g

Sodium: 1.4 mg
Diabetic exchanges
  Starch: ½
  Fat: 2

Wheat Germ Topping

½ cup all-purpose flour
3 tablespoons wheat germ
½ teaspoon cinnamon
2 tablespoons vegetable oil

Optional: ¼ cup unsweetened coconut,
  premoistened with 1 teaspoon
  water and 1 teaspoon vegetable oil;
  or ¼ cup seeds; *or* ¼ cup chopped
  nuts

1. In a medium-sized bowl, mix all ingredients with a fork.
2. Spoon topping over any pie or fruit mixture and smooth topping by hand.

Yield: Enough topping for one crisp or one 9-inch pie (8.5 servings)

PER SERVING

Calories: 68
Protein: 1.6 g
Fat: 3.5 g
Carbohydrate: 7.5 g

Sodium: 0.3 mg
Diabetic exchanges
  Starch: ½
  Fat: ¾

Whole-Wheat 'n' Walnut Topping

¾ cup whole-wheat flour
¼ cup chopped walnuts
¼ cup rolled oats

Generous ¼ teaspoon cinnamon
5 tablespoons vegetable shortening or
lard

1. In a medium-sized bowl, mix all ingredients with a fork.
2. Spoon topping over any pie or fruit mixture and smooth topping by hand.

Yield: Enough topping for one crisp or one 9-inch pie (8.5 servings)

PER SERVING

Calories: 131
Protein: 2.7 g
Fat: 10.1 g
Carbohydrate: 9.6 g

Sodium: 0.4 mg
Diabetic exchanges
  Starch: ½
  Fat: 2

Whole-Wheat and Sesame Topping

¾ cup whole-wheat flour
1 to 2 tablespoons sesame seeds
4 tablespoons vegetable shortening or
lard
¼ to ½ teaspoon cinnamon

Optional: ⅓ cup unsweetened coconut,
premoistened with 1½ teaspoons
water and 1½ teaspoons vegetable
oil; *or* ⅓ cup seeds; *or* ⅓ cup chopped
nuts; *or* ⅓ cup rolled oats

1. In a medium-sized bowl, mix all ingredients with a fork.
2. Spoon topping over any pie or fruit mixture and smooth topping by hand.

Yield: Enough topping for one crisp or one 9-inch pie (8.5 servings)

PER SERVING

Calories: 93
Protein: 1.6 g
Fat: 6.9 g
Carbohydrate: 7.7 g

Sodium: 0.7 mg
Diabetic exchanges
  Starch: ½
  Fat: 1¼

FRUIT
SAUCES
AND
FRUIT
PUDDINGS

Puddings are versatile and delicious nonsugar treats. They can be served plain, with a sprinkling of unsweetened coconut or nuts or seeds, or they can be used as a pie filling in any prebaked pie crust.

The secret to making creamy, smooth pudding is to stir constantly once the thickener has been added. You must also make sure that you cook the pudding long enough for it to become thick. Pudding will usually splatter when it boils, so use a cover with vents, or only partially cover the saucepan.

THICKENERS

Arrowroot. This is my favorite thickener because it does not affect the taste of the pudding the way flour often does. When cooked over medium heat, arrowroot will thicken your fruit mixture *before* it reaches the boiling point, so make sure that you watch the mixture, stir constantly, and are careful not to overcook.

Cornstarch. Use this only if you are not allergic to corn. When cooked over medium heat, cornstarch will thicken your fruit mixture one to two minutes after it reaches the boiling point. Be sure to stir constantly during the entire cooking time.

Flour. Flour may add its own flavor to your puddings. When cooked over medium heat, flour will thicken your fruit mixture two to three minutes after it reaches the boiling point. Be sure to stir constantly during the entire cooking time.

Minute Tapioca. Tapioca is similar to arrowroot in that it does not affect the taste of the fruit in your pudding. You should combine tapioca with fruit and concentrate in a small saucepan and allow to stand for five minutes. Stirring constantly, bring to a boil over medium heat. Boil one minute. Remove from heat and cool. Pudding thickens as it cools.

Equivalents

    2 tablespoons flour = 1 tablespoon arrowroot

    2 tablespoons flour = 1 tablespoon cornstarch

    1 tablespoon cornstarch = 2 tablespoons Minute tapioca

Raspberry Tapioca Pudding

2 cups fresh or frozen, thawed, and
 drained raspberries
2 tablespoons Minute tapioca

½ cup unsweetened apple juice
 concentrate (any brand)

1. Puree berries in a blender and press through a strainer to remove seeds.
2. Combine all ingredients in a small saucepan and allow to sit for 5 minutes.
3. Place saucepan over medium heat and bring mixture to a boil, stirring constantly. Continue boiling and stirring for 1 minute, then remove pan from heat and allow mixture to cool for 20 minutes before stirring well and spooning into small bowls or parfait glasses.
4. Chill in refrigerator for 3 hours before serving.

Yield: 4 servings

PER SERVING

Calories: 108
Protein: 0.7 g
Fat: 0.5 g
Carbohydrate: 26.6 g

Sodium: 8.8 mg
Diabetic exchanges
 Fruit: 2

Apple or Pear Pudding Sauce

3 apples or pears, peeled, cored, and sliced
⅓ cup unsweetened apple juice concentrate (any brand)
Generous ½ teaspoon cinnamon
¾ cup water (if necessary, add ⅛ cup additional water while mixture is cooking to retain puddinglike consistency)
1 tablespoon plus 1 teaspoon all-purpose flour

1. In a medium-sized saucepan, combine fruit, concentrate, cinnamon, and water. Place saucepan over medium heat and bring mixture to a boil. Reduce heat and simmer until tender—about 45 minutes—stirring occasionally. Remove pan from heat, mash mixture, and allow it to cool slightly.

2. Add flour, return saucepan to medium heat, and bring mixture to a boil, stirring constantly. Continue to cook and stir at a light boil for 2 to 3 minutes. Remove pan from heat and allow mixture to cool.

3. Serve plain. Refrigerate or freeze in an airtight container.

Yield: 4 servings

PER SERVING

Calories: 103
Protein: 0.5 g
Fat: 0.4 g
Carbohydrate: 25.9 g
Sodium: 5.9 mg
Diabetic exchanges
 Fruit: 2

Quick Apple or Pear Pudding

4 cups peeled, cored, and sliced apples
   or pears
⅓ cup unsweetened apple juice
   concentrate (any brand)
½ teaspoon cinnamon

2 tablespoons plus ½ teaspoon
   arrowroot or cornstarch
Chopped nuts or unsweetened coconut
   (optional)

1. Puree fruit and concentrate in a blender.

2. In a medium-sized saucepan, combine fruit mixture and cinnamon. Place saucepan over medium heat and bring mixture to a boil. Partially cover to allow steam to escape, reduce heat, and simmer for 10 minutes, stirring occasionally. Be careful to avoid splatters.

3. Remove pan from heat and let mixture cool.

4. When mixture is cool, add arrowroot (or cornstarch), place saucepan over medium heat, and stir constantly. Arrowroot will thicken the mixture before it reaches the boiling point. (Cornstarch will thicken it 1 to 2 minutes after it reaches the boiling point.)

5. When mixture reaches desired pudding consistency, remove pan from heat and let cool for 15 minutes. Stir mixture, pour into serving bowls, cover, and refrigerate until ready to serve. Serve plain or topped with chopped nuts or moistened unsweetened coconut, if desired. (Coconut can be premoistened with a little water and vegetable oil. Just mix and let coconut soak up moisture for a few minutes before sprinkling on pudding.) If you are going to stir coconut into the pudding, do not moisten the coconut.

Yield: 4 servings

PER SERVING

Calories: 117
Protein: 0.3 g
Fat: 0.4 g
Carbohydrate: 29.9 g

Sodium: 6.0 mg
Diabetic exchanges
   Fruit: 2

Apple or Pear or Peach Sauce

4 pieces fruit (apples, pears, or
   peaches), peeled, cored, and sliced
Scant ½ teaspoon cinnamon
½ cup unsweetened apple juice
   concentrate (any brand)

½ cup water (if necessary, add ⅛ to ¼
   cup additional water while mixture
   is cooking to retain puddinglike
   consistency)

1. In a medium-sized saucepan, combine all ingredients. Place saucepan over medium heat and bring mixture to a boil. Reduce heat and simmer for 45 minutes, stirring occasionally, until fruit is soft and cooked through.

2. Remove pan from heat and allow mixture to cool for 20 minutes.

3. With a fork or potato masher, mash fruit to sauce consistency, pour into container, and refrigerate until ready to use.

Yield: 4 servings

PER SERVING (USING APPLES FOR FRUIT)

Calories: 132
Protein: 0.4 g
Fat: 0.5 g
Carbohydrate: 33.5 g

Sodium: 8.9 mg
Diabetic exchanges
   Fruit: 2

Fast-and-Easy Fruit Sauce

3 cups peeled and sliced fruit of choice
   (apple, pear, peach, plum, or nectarine)
1/3 cup unsweetened apple juice
   concentrate (any brand) or water

Scant 1/2 teaspoon cinnamon
Chopped nuts or unsweetened coconut
   (optional)

1. Puree fruit and concentrate (or water) in blender.

2. In a medium-sized saucepan, combine fruit mixture and cinnamon. Place saucepan over medium heat and bring to a boil. Partially cover to allow steam to escape, reduce heat, and simmer for 10 minutes, stirring occasionally. Be careful to avoid splatters.

3. Remove pan from heat and let mixture cool. Serve immediately, plain or topped with chopped nuts or moistened unsweetened coconut (coconut can be premoistened with a little water and vegetable oil; just mix and let coconut soak up moisture for a few minutes before sprinkling on pudding). If you are going to stir coconut into the sauce, do not moisten the coconut. Pour sauce into container, cover, and refrigerate if not serving immediately.

Yield: 4 servings

PER SERVING (USING ONE CUP EACH OF APPLE, PEAR, AND PEACH)

Calories: 98
Protein: 0.6 g
Fat: 0.4 g
Carbohydrate: 24.8 g

Sodium: 5.9 mg
Diabetic exchanges
  Fruit: 1 1/2

Pineapple-Nut Pudding

One 20-ounce can unsweetened
   pineapple chunks (use Dole if you
   are allergic to phenol)
2 tablespoons unsweetened apple juice
   concentrate (any brand)
1 tablespoon plus 1 teaspoon arrowroot
   or cornstarch

2 tablespoons *dry* unsweetened
   coconut, sesame seeds, or poppy
   seeds
⅛ teaspoon cinnamon
2 tablespoons chopped pecans

1. Measure ¾ cup pineapple chunks, drain, reserving juice, and pat dry. Set aside.

2. Place remaining pineapple chunks and all the juice from the can in a blender. Add apple juice concentrate and blend.

3. In a medium-sized saucepan, combine pineapple puree and arrowroot (or cornstarch). Place saucepan over medium heat and stir constantly. Arrowroot will thicken the mixture before it reaches the boiling point. (Cornstarch will thicken it 1 to 2 minutes after it reaches the boiling point.)

4. When mixture reaches desired pudding consistency, remove from heat, add ¾ cup dry pineapple chunks, coconut, cinnamon, and pecans. Stir, cool for 20 minutes, stir again, and pour into four small bowls. Cover and refrigerate until ready to serve.

Yield: 4 servings

PER SERVING

Calories: 150
Protein: 1.1 g
Fat. 4.2 g
Carbohydrate: 29.6 g

Sodium: 4.6 mg
Diabetic exchanges
   Fat: 1
   Fruit: 2

Quick Peach Pudding

4 cups peeled, pitted, and chopped
   peaches
½ cup unsweetened apple juice
   concentrate (any brand)

½ teaspoon cinnamon
4 tablespoons arrowroot or cornstarch
Chopped nuts or unsweetened coconut
   (optional)

1. Puree peaches and concentrate in a blender.

2. In a medium-sized saucepan, combine fruit mixture and cinnamon. Place saucepan over medium heat and bring to a boil. Partially cover to allow steam to escape, reduce heat, and simmer for 10 minutes, stirring occasionally. Be careful to avoid splatters.

3. Remove pan from heat and let mixture cool.

4. When mixture is cool, add arrowroot (or cornstarch), place saucepan over medium heat, and stir constantly. Arrowroot will thicken the mixture before it reaches the boiling point. (Cornstarch will thicken it 1 to 2 minutes after it reaches the boiling point.)

5. When mixture reaches desired pudding consistency, remove pan from heat and let mixture cool for 15 minutes. Stir mixture, pour into serving bowls, cover, and refrigerate until ready to serve. Serve plain or top with chopped nuts or moistened unsweetened coconut (coconut can be premoistened with a little water and vegetable oil; just mix and let coconut absorb moisture for a few minutes before sprinkling on pudding). If you are going to stir coconut into the pudding, do not moisten the coconut.

Yield: 4 servings

PER SERVING

Calories: 161
Protein: 1.4 g
Fat: 0.3 g
Carbohydrate: 40.6 g

Sodium: 9.0 mg
Diabetic exchanges
  Fruit: 2½

Baked Apples

2 large washed and cored baking
   apples, such as McIntosh,
   Jonathan or Cortland (see *Note*)
16 raisins, divided, optional
¼ cup water
¼ cup unsweetened apple juice
   concentrate (any brand)

1 teaspoon vegetable oil
1 tablespoon brown-rice syrup,
   optional (Sweet Dreams Brown
   Rice Syrup by Lundberg; make sure
   label states ''Gluten-Free'')
Sprinkles of cinnamon

1. Preheat oven to 325°F.

2. Place apples in a baking dish with lid. Place 8 raisins inside each apple, if desired.

3. In a small bowl, mix water, concentrate, oil, and brown-rice syrup. Pour over apples in baking dish. Sprinkle apples with cinnamon.

4. Bake 45 to 55 minutes, covered, until apples are tender; time will vary depending on size and type of apple.

5. To serve, spoon baked apples into pretty dessert bowls and top with liquid from baking dish. Serve hot or cold.

Yield: 2 servings

PER SERVING

Calories: 203
Protein: 0.6 g
Fat: 3.2 g
Carbohydrate: 46.8 g

Sodium: 8.8 mg
Diabetic exchanges
  Fat: ½
  Fruit: 3

Note: Thicker skinned apples, such as Red Delicious, should be peeled.

COOKIES, BARS, AND CANDIES

Yes, it's possible to create great-tasting candies and cookies without using refined sugar or honey. By substituting fruit concentrates, date sugar, or brown-rice syrup, you can turn out sweet treats that the whole family will enjoy. Brown-rice syrup can be found in most health-food stores; one brand I use is Westbrae Natural Brown Rice Syrup; another brand is Sweet Dreams Brown Rice Syrup made by Lundberg. For people with celiac disease (intolerance to gluten) make sure label states "Gluten-Free."

Sugar-Free, Dairy-Free Fudge

¼ cup water
2 ounces (2 squares) Baker's All
   Natural Unsweetened Chocolate
1 tablespoon vegetable oil
½ cup plus 2 tablespoons date sugar

¼ cup brown-rice syrup (Westbrae
   Natural Brown Rice Syrup; make
   sure label states "Gluten-Free")
Generous ½ cup chopped English
   walnuts or nut of choice

1. Place water, chocolate, and oil in a medium-sized saucepan. Cook, stirring constantly, over medium heat until melted.

2. Add date sugar to melted chocolate and continue cooking over medium heat for 1 minute.

3. Remove saucepan from burner, add brown rice syrup, and return pan to stove. Continue cooking on medium heat, stirring constantly, for 2 minutes. Turn burner down to low heat the last 30 seconds of cooking time.

4. Take saucepan off burner and add the chopped nuts. Stir.

5. Cool for 3 to 4 minutes. Using spoons, place 17 portions of mixture on waxed paper to cool for 2 minutes, or until cool enough to handle.

6. Roll each portion in palms of hands to form 17 balls. Freeze balls in a container with lid. Remove balls from freezer a few minutes before serving.

Yield: 17 balls

PER BALL

Calories: 74
Protein: 0.9 g
Fat: 4.8 g
Carbohydrate: 8.4 g

Sodium: 12 mg
Diabetic exchanges
  Starch: ½
  Fat: 1

Chocolate Nut Balls

1 ounce (1 square) Baker's All-Natural
   Unsweetened Chocolate
1 tablespoon vegetable oil

5 tablespoons water
½ cup date sugar
¾ cup chopped pecans or nuts of choice

1. In a small saucepan, melt chocolate, oil, and water over medium heat.

2. Reduce heat to low, add date sugar, and cook, stirring, for 2 to 3 minutes. The mixture will become quite a bit thicker. The date sugar will become softer and blend into the mixture.

3. Remove pan from heat and add the chopped nuts. Stir well.

4. Drop chocolate mixture by heaping spoonfuls into 11 portions on an *unoiled* 9- by 9-inch glass dish. Let balls cool. To store, place nut balls in a covered container and refrigerate or freeze.

Yield: 11 balls

PER BALL (USING PECANS FOR CHOPPED NUTS)

Calories: 100
Protein: 0.9 g
Fat: 8.2 g
Carbohydrate: 7.7 g

Sodium: 0.4 mg
Diabetic exchanges
  Starch: ½
  Fat: 1.5

Coco-Nut Fudge Balls

1½ cups date sugar
¼ cup unsweetened purple grape juice concentrate (any brand)
¼ cup unsweetened apple juice concentrate (any brand)
2 tablespoons vegetable oil
2 ounces (2 squares) Baker's Unsweetened All-Natural Chocolate

5 tablespoons water
2 egg whites
¾ cup chopped nuts
Garnish: ⅓ to ⅔ cup chopped nuts *and/or* ⅓ to ⅔ cup unsweetened coconut, premoistened with 1¼ teaspoons water and 1¼ teaspoons vegetable oil

1. In a medium-sized saucepan, combine all ingredients except egg whites, nuts, and garnish. Place saucepan over medium heat and cook for 2 minutes, stirring constantly so mixture will not burn. Remove saucepan from heat and let mixture cool for 3 to 5 minutes.

2. Beat in egg whites, return saucepan to medium heat, and cook, stirring, until mixture is thick. Remove saucepan from heat and stir in ¾ cup chopped nuts.

3. Pour mixture into an 8- by 8- by 2-inch pan and freeze for 1 hour.

4. Remove pan from freezer. Using your fingers, place a small portion of the mixture in the palm of your hand and roll into a 1-inch ball. Repeat to form 12 balls.

5. Roll balls in garnish. Freeze in an airtight container until ready to serve (fudge tastes best frozen). Aging in the freezer for 2 to 3 weeks enhances the flavor of the fudge.

Yield: 12 balls

PER BALL (USING PECANS FOR CHOPPED NUTS)

Calories: 176
Protein: 2.2 g
Fat: 9.6 g
Carbohydrate: 22.8 g
Sodium: 12.4 mg

Diabetic exchanges
Starch: ½
Fat: 2
Fruit: 1

Space Balls

⅓ cup chopped (cut with scissors) and packed dates

⅓ cup *dry* unsweetened coconut

¼ cup packed raisins

⅓ cup chopped (cut with scissors) and packed dried Calimyrna figs

⅓ cup chopped pecans

2 tablespoons brown-rice syrup (Westbrae Natural Brown Rice Syrup; make sure label states "Gluten-Free")

Generous ½ cup unsweetened coconut, premoistened with 1½ teaspoons water and 1½ teaspoons vegetable oil

1. In a large bowl, stir together all ingredients except brown-rice syrup and premoistened coconut.

2. Stir in brown-rice syrup 1 tablespoon at a time.

3. Roll mixture into 8 balls, shaping firmly.

4. Roll balls in premoistened coconut. To store, place balls in an airtight container and refrigerate or freeze.

Yield: 8 balls

PER BALL

Calories: 132

Protein: 1.2 g

Fat: 7.2 g

Carbohydrate: 18.1 g

Sodium: 3.9 mg

Diabetic exchanges

  Fat: 1½

  Fruit: 1¼

Chocolate-Dipped Pecan Dates

20 large pitted dates
Approximately ¼ cup pecan pieces
¼ cup water
2 ounces (2 squares) Baker's All-
Natural Unsweetened Chocolate

1 tablespoon vegetable oil
½ cup plus 2 tablespoons date sugar
¼ cup brown-rice syrup (Westbrae
Natural Brown Rice Syrup; make
sure label states "Gluten-Free")

1. Stuff dates with pecan pieces, enlarging ends of dates with a knife if necessary.

2. In a medium-sized saucepan, combine water, chocolate, and oil. Place saucepan over medium heat until chocolate is melted, stirring constantly.

3. Add date sugar to melted chocolate mixture and continue stirring over medium heat for 1 minute.

4. Add rice syrup and continue stirring over medium heat until mixture starts to become gooey—1 to 2 minutes. Remove saucepan from heat and allow mixture to cool for 1 to 2 minutes.

5. Using a large metal spoon, dip each date in chocolate mixture until completely coated, then place on waxed paper.

6. When all dates are coated, if you have chocolate left over in saucepan, spoon excess evenly over cooling dates. As the mixture cools, the chocolate will become less gooey. Roll each one between your palms until chocolate is smooth and date is completely covered.

7. Wrap each date in a small piece of plastic wrap, twisting ends of wrap. Place wrapped dates in a large plastic bag and freeze until ready to serve. Let thaw 10 to 15 minutes before serving.

Yield: 20 dates

PER DATE

Calories: 82
Protein: 0.9 g
Fat: 4.1 g
Carbohydrate: 12.1 g

Sodium: 0.6 mg
Diabetic exchanges
  Fat: ¾
  Fruit: ¾

Banana-Coconut Bars

⅓ cup vegetable oil
Generous 1 cup mashed banana
4 egg whites *or* 2 extralarge eggs
½ cup water or milk
1¾ cups all-purpose flour
1 cup unsweetened coconut,
  premoistened with 2½ to 2¾
  teaspoons water and 2½ to 2¾
  teaspoons vegetable oil

1 teaspoon baking soda
2¼ teaspoons baking powder
½ cup unsweetened coconut,
  premoistened with 1¼ to 1½
  teaspoons water and 1¼ to 1½
  teaspoons vegetable oil (for topping)

1. Preheat oven to 350°F. Oil and flour a 13- by 9- by 2-inch baking pan.

2. Combine all ingredients except baking soda, baking powder, and ½ cup coconut in a large bowl and beat well by hand.

3. Stir in baking soda and baking powder quickly, and then mix (28 to 30 beats); immediately pour mixture into prepared baking pan.

4. Quickly sprinkle ½ cup coconut on batter and bake 20 to 22 minutes, or until a toothpick inserted in center comes out clean.

5. Remove pan from oven and let mixture cool in pan. Cut into 15 bars. To store, place cooled bars in an airtight container and refrigerate, freeze, or store on countertop.

Yield: 15 bars

PER BAR

Calories: 152	*Sodium:* 119.2 mg
Protein: 2.7 g	*Diabetic exchanges*
Fat: 9.0 g	Starch: 1
Carbohydrate: 15.5 g	Fat: 1¾

Banana-Coconut Bars

No Egg

⅓ cup vegetable oil

Generous 1 cup mashed banana

½ cup water

1¾ cups all-purpose flour

¼ cup water

1 tablespoon egg replacer (Ener-G brand)

1 cup unsweetened coconut, premoistened with 1 tablespoon water and 1 tablespoon vegetable oil

1 teaspoon baking soda

2½ teaspoons baking powder

½ cup unsweetened coconut, premoistened with 1½ teaspoons water and 1½ teaspoons vegetable oil (for topping)

1. Preheat oven to 350°F. Oil and flour a 13- by 9- by 2-inch baking pan.

2. In a large bowl, combine ⅓ cup oil, banana, and water; beat by hand for 45 seconds. Add flour and beat for 2 minutes.

3. In a small bowl, and using a hand-operated mechanical beater, beat together water and egg replacer until bubbles form (mixture should not be thick or stiff). Pour egg-replacer mixture into banana mixture and stir for 20 seconds by hand. Stir in 1 cup of premoistened coconut. Stir in baking soda and baking powder quickly, and then mix (28 to 30 beats); immediately pour mixture into prepared baking pan. Sprinkle remaining ½ cup coconut evenly over batter.

4. Bake about 23 minutes, or until a toothpick inserted in center comes out clean.

5. Remove pan from oven and let mixture cool in pan. Cut into 15 bars. To store, place cooled bars in an airtight container and refrigerate, freeze, or store on countertop.

Yield: 15 bars

PER BAR

Calories: 143

Protein: 1.9 g

Fat: 8.3 g

Carbohydrate: 15.6 g

Sodium: 110.9 mg

Diabetic exchanges

    Starch: 1

    Fat: 1½

Banana-Oat-Coconut Bars

No Egg

1 cup oat flour

1 cup Ener-G brand oat mix (see *Note*)

½ cup unsweetened coconut, premoistened with 1¼ teaspoons water and 1¼ teaspoons vegetable oil

¼ teaspoon salt

3½ teaspoons baking powder

1 teaspoon baking soda

½ teaspoon cinnamon

¼ teaspoon nutmeg

Generous 1 cup mashed banana

4 tablespoons oat flour

3 tablespoons vegetable oil

4 tablespoons water

¼ cup unsweetened coconut, premoistened with ¾ teaspoon water and ¾ teaspoon vegetable oil (for topping)

1. Preheat oven to 350°F. Oil a 9- by 9- by 2-inch baking pan.

2. In a large bowl and using a fork, stir together the 1 cup oat flour, 1 cup oat mix, ½ cup coconut, salt, baking powder, baking soda, cinnamon, and nutmeg.

3. In a medium-sized bowl, combine banana, 4 tablespoons oat flour, oil, and water. Beat with a hand-operated mechanical beater until well mixed.

4. Add banana mixture to oat-flour mixture and stir quickly (28 to 30 beats). Pour batter quickly into prepared pan and sprinkle with ¼ cup premoistened coconut.

5. Bake 30 to 35 minutes, or until knife inserted in center comes out clean.

6. Remove pan from oven and cool on a wire rack. Cut into 9 bars. To store, place cooled bars in an airtight container and refrigerate, freeze, or store on countertop.

Yield: 9 bars

PER BAR

Calories: 204	*Sodium:* 276.0 mg
Protein: 4.7 g	*Diabetic exchanges*
Fat: 10.2 g	*Starch:* 1½
Carbohydrate: 25.4 g	*Fat:* 2

Note: You may substitute 1 cup regular oat flour for 1 cup Ener-G brand oat mix, in which case you must add an additional ½ teaspoon baking powder.

Sweet Date Bars

1 cup raisins
¾ cup plus 2 tablespoons date sugar
½ cup crushed and drained
   unsweetened pineapple (use Dole
   if you are allergic to phenol)
2 teaspoons pineapple juice from can
1¼ cups unsweetened apple juice
   concentrate (any brand)
⅓ cup plus 1 tablespoon vegetable oil
1½ cups plus 2 tablespoons all-purpose
   flour

4 egg whites *or* 2 extralarge eggs,
   beaten
¼ cup unsweetened coconut,
   premoistened with ½ to ¾
   teaspoon water and ½ to ¾ teaspoon
   vegetable oil
¾ cup chopped nuts
1 teaspoon cinnamon
¼ teaspoon nutmeg
1½ teaspoons baking soda

1. Preheat oven to 350°F. Oil and flour a 13- by 9- by 2-inch baking pan.

2. In a medium-sized saucepan, combine raisins, date sugar, pineapple, pineapple juice, and apple juice concentrate. Place saucepan over medium heat, bring mixture to a boil, and boil for 3 minutes, stirring frequently.

3. Remove saucepan from heat, add oil, stir, and let cool.

4. In a medium-sized bowl, stir together flour, eggs, coconut, chopped nuts, cinnamon, and nutmeg.

5. Add cooled pineapple mixture to flour mixture and stir well for 2 minutes. Stir in baking soda quickly and then mix (28 to 30 beats); immediately pour batter into prepared pan.

6. Bake about 34 minutes, or until bars pull away slightly from sides of pan and feel firm to the touch.

7. Remove pan from oven and let mixture cool in pan. Slice into bars. To store, place cooled bars in an airtight container and refrigerate or freeze.

Yield: 15 bars

PER BAR (USING PECANS FOR CHOPPED NUTS)

Calories: 258
Protein: 3.8 g
Fat: 10.7 g
Carbohydrate: 38.7 g
Sodium: 149 mg

Diabetic exchanges
  Starch: 2
  Fat: 2
  Fruit: ½

Fig-Nut Bars

No Egg

¼ cup vegetable oil

¼ cup unsweetened apple juice concentrate (any brand)

½ cup plus 2 tablespoons plus ½ teaspoon water

1½ teaspoons pure potato-starch flour

1½ cups plus 1 tablespoon all-purpose flour

½ cup chopped (cut with scissors) and packed dried Calimyrna figs

10 chopped (cut with scissors) dried Black Mission figs

⅓ cup chopped pecans

2 tablespoons sesame seeds

2 tablespoons water

1½ teaspoons egg replacer (Ener-G brand)

1 teaspoon baking soda

2½ teaspoons baking powder

¼ cup chopped pecans (for topping)

1. Preheat oven to 350°F. Oil and flour a 9- by 9- by 2-inch baking pan.

2. In a large bowl, stir together oil, concentrate, water, and potato-starch flour. Add all-purpose flour and beat for 2 minutes by hand. Add Calimyrna and Black Mission figs, ⅓ cup pecans, and sesame seeds and beat for 2 minutes by hand.

3. In a small bowl, and using a hand-operated mechanical beater, beat together water and egg replacer until bubbles form (mixture should not be thick or stiff). Pour egg-replacer mixture into fig mixture and stir for 20 seconds by hand. Stir in baking soda and baking powder quickly, and then mix (28 to 30 beats); immediately pour mixture into prepared baking pan. Quickly sprinkle ¼ cup chopped pecans evenly over top.

4. Bake 35 minutes, or until a cake tester inserted in center comes out clean.

5. Remove pan from oven and cool on a wire rack. Cut into bars. To store, place cooled bars in an airtight container and refrigerate or freeze.

Yield: 9 bars

PER BAR

Calories: 281

Protein: 4.1 g

Fat: 12.7 g

Carbohydrate: 39.3 g

Sodium: 189.2 mg

Diabetic exchanges

Starch: 1½

Fat: 2½

Fruit: 1

Granola Bars

2½ cups rolled oats
¼ cup sesame seeds
⅛ cup raw hulled sunflower seeds
½ cup raw wheat germ
½ cup unsweetened coconut,
  premoistened with 1½ teaspoons
  water and 1½ teaspoons vegetable
  oil
¾ cup chopped pecans

1 cup chopped (cut with scissors) and
  packed raisins, dates, and dried figs
  (any combination)
2 tablespoons vegetable oil
Generous ¾ cup brown-rice syrup
  (Sweet Dreams Brown Rice Syrup
  by Lundberg)

1. Preheat oven to 275°F. Oil a 15- by 10- by ½-inch baking pan.

2. In a large bowl, mix together all ingredients with a fork. Pour into prepared baking pan. Dampen hands with water and press down firmly on the dough, leaving a 10- by 1-inch rectangle of pan bottom uncovered so that you can use a spatula to test the bottom of the mixture for doneness.

3. Bake about 31 minutes, or until bottoms of bars show just a *hint* of color change. (Bars will get crisper as they cool so don't let bottom become golden.)

4. Remove pan from oven and place on a wire rack to cool for 10 to 15 minutes. Use a knife to cut into bars. To store, place cooled bars in an airtight container and refrigerate or freeze.

Yield: 18 bars

PER BAR (USING ONLY RAISINS FOR CHOPPED FRUIT)

Calories: 180
Protein: 4.4 g
Fat: 8.7 g
Carbohydrate: 23.6 g
Sodium: 3.6 mg

Diabetic exchanges
  Starch: 1
  Fat: 1½
  Fruit: ½

Dried-Fruit Granola Bars

No Oatmeal or Wheat

½ cup chopped (cut with scissors) and
    packed dried Calimyrna figs
½ cup chopped (cut with scissors) and
    packed dates
½ cup packed raisins
½ cup chopped (cut with scissors) and
    packed prunes
¼ cup sesame seeds

1½ cups chopped pecans
¼ cup raw, hulled sunflower seeds
½ cup unsweetened coconut,
    premoistened with 1 tablespoon
    water and 1 tablespoon vegetable oil
¼ cup brown-rice syrup (Westbrae
    Natural Brown Rice Syrup; make
    sure label states "Gluten-Free")

1. Preheat oven to 275°F. Oil an 8- by 8- by 2-inch baking pan.

2. In a large bowl, combine all ingredients. Pour into prepared baking pan. Dampen hands with water and press down firmly on dough.

3. Bake for 28 minutes, or until bars become nearly dry and less sticky to the touch. (Bars will get firmer as they cool, so be careful not to overcook.)

4. Remove pan from oven and place on a wire rack to cool for 20 minutes. With a down-up motion, use a spatula to cut into 9 bars. Leave bars in pan and refrigerate, uncovered, until completely cooled. To serve, remove bars with a spatula and place on a serving plate. To store, place cooled bars in an airtight container and refrigerate or freeze.

Yield: 9 bars

PER BAR

Calories: 321
Protein: 4.3 g
Fat: 20.7 g
Carbohydrate: 34.8 g

Sodium: 5.8 mg
Diabetic exchanges
  Fat: 4
  Fruit: 2¼

Whole-Wheat Raisin Cookies

1¼ cups all-purpose flour
1¼ cups 100% stone-ground whole-
  wheat flour
½ teaspoon salt
1½ teaspoons baking soda
1½ cups date sugar

1½ cups raisins
⅓ cup vegetable oil
½ cup plus generous 2 tablespoons
  water
4 egg whites or 2 extralarge eggs

1. Preheat oven to 350°F. Grease two cookie sheets with vegetable shortening or oil.

2. In a large-sized bowl, stir together flours, salt, baking soda, date sugar, and raisins. Set aside.

3. In a medium-sized bowl, combine oil, water, and eggs. Beat mixture for 30 to 40 seconds with a hand-operated mechanical beater. Add to flour-date mixture, stirring until ingredients are well moistened and raisins are distributed in cookie dough. Quickly place batter onto prepared cookie sheets by large tablespoonfuls.

4. Bake 10 minutes, or until there is just a hint of light brown on cookie bottoms. Rotate cookie sheets at the halfway point to achieve even baking.

5. Remove pans from oven; remove cookies from pans and place on a countertop until completely cool. To store, place cookies in an airtight container and store on countertop or freeze.

Yield: 35 cookies

PER COOKIE

Calories: 93
Protein: 1.7 g
Fat: 2.2 g
Carbohydrate: 17.3 g

Sodium: 91.8 mg
Diabetic exchanges
  Starch: 1
  Fat: ½

Chocolate-Date Cookies

No Egg

2 cups all-purpose flour, tapped lightly
    4 to 5 times
1 cup packed date sugar
¼ cup plus 1 tablespoon unsweetened
    cocoa powder or unsweetened
    carob powder (see page 00)
½ teaspoon salt

⅓ cup vegetable oil
¼ cup unsweetened purple grape juice
    concentrate (Welch's)
¼ cup unsweetened apple juice
    concentrate (any brand)
1 cup plus 1 tablespoon water
1½ teaspoons baking soda

1. Preheat oven to 350°F. Grease two cookie sheets with vegetable shortening or oil.

2. In a large bowl, stir together flour, date sugar, cocoa, and salt. Set aside.

3. In a medium-sized bowl, combine oil, concentrates, and water. Beat mixture for 30 seconds with a hand-operated mechanical beater. Add concentrate mixture to flour mixture and beat well, by hand, for 4 minutes. Stir in baking soda quickly, and then mix (28 to 30 beats); quickly place batter by heaping tablespoonfuls onto prepared cookie sheets.

4. Bake 12 minutes, or until cookies look dry. Rotate cookie sheets at the half-way point to achieve even baking.

5. Remove pans from oven; remove cookies from pans and place on a countertop until completely cool. To store, place cookies in an airtight container and refrigerate or freeze.

Yield: 28 to 30 cookies

PER COOKIE

Calories: 83
Protein: 1.1 g
Fat: 2.8 g
Carbohydrate: 13.8 g

Sodium: 107 mg
Diabetic exchanges
   Starch: 1
   Fat: ½

Giant Spelt Carob Chip Cookies

Has Gluten

If you want crunchy cookies, use ⅓ cup oil and bake about 14 minutes. If you want softer cookies, use a generous ⅓ cup oil and bake about 16 minutes.

2½ cups plus 1 tablespoon spelt whole-grain flour, tapped lightly 4 to 5 times
½ teaspoon salt
1½ teaspoons baking soda
1½ cups date sugar

⅓ cup to generous ⅓ cup vegetable oil
¼ cup plus generous 2 tablespoons water
4 egg whites or 2 extralarge eggs
Generous 1 cup milk-free, sugar-free carob drops

1. Preheat oven to 350°F. Oil a large cookie sheet.

2. In a small-sized bowl, stir together flour, salt, and baking soda.

3. In a large-sized bowl, combine date sugar, oil, water, and eggs. Beat ingredients together by hand for 3 minutes, removing lumps and blending mixture well.

4. Pour flour mixture a little at a time into date sugar mixture, stirring after each addition. Dough will be quite thick. Add carob drops and mix.

5. Using a ¼-cup measuring cup as a mold, drop batter onto prepared cookie sheet. All cookies should be approximately the same shape and size. You should get 13 giant cookies in all.

6. Place cookie sheet on next to bottom rack in oven. Bake 14 to 16 minutes, depending on amount of oil used in recipe. When done, cookies should look dry and not be mushy to the touch. The cookies will be dark brown on the bottom and have a tinge of brown in a few spots on top.

7. Remove pans from oven; remove cookies from pans and place on a countertop until completely cool. To store, place cooled cookies in an airtight container and store on countertop or freeze.

Yield: 13 giant cookies

PER COOKIE

Calories: 225	*Sodium:* 244 mg
Protein: 5.6 g	*Diabetic exchanges*
Fat: 7.9 g	*Starch:* 2½
Carbohydrate: 38.2 g	*Fat:* 1

Quick-Change Cookie

This cookie can be made three different ways. The plain recipe creates a nice, pleasant-tasting, soft cookie. Add milk-free, sugar-free carob drops and you have Carob Chip Cookies. Or, you can flavor the batter with grated chocolate for a Mild Chocolate Cookie. (See Carob Chip Cookie and Mild Chocolate Cookie variations.)

2½ cups all-purpose flour, tapped lightly 4 to 5 times
½ teaspoon salt
1½ teaspoons baking soda
1½ cups date sugar

⅓ cup vegetable oil
½ cup plus 1 tablespoon plus 1 teaspoon water
4 egg whites or 2 extralarge eggs

1. Preheat oven to 350°F. Grease two cookie sheets with vegetable shortening or oil.

2. In a medium-sized bowl, stir together flour, salt, and baking soda.

3. In a large-sized bowl, combine date sugar, oil, water, and eggs. Beat mixture well by hand for 3 minutes. Add flour mixture, a third at a time, to date sugar mixture, stirring well after each addition.

4. Quickly drop batter by large tablespoonfuls onto prepared cookie sheets.

5. Bake 9 minutes, or until cookies are firm. Rotate cookie sheets at the halfway point to achieve even baking.

6. Remove pans from oven; remove cookies from pans and place on a countertop until completely cool. To store, place cookies in an airtight container and store on countertop or freeze.

Yield: 31 cookies

PER COOKIE (PLAIN RECIPE)

Calories: 83
Protein: 1.5 g
Fat: 2.4 g
Carbohydrate: 13.5 g

Sodium: 103 mg
Diabetic exchanges
  Starch: 1
  Fat: ½

CAROB CHIP COOKIE: Add 1 cup milk-free, sugar-free carob drops to the date sugar mixture in step 3. Continue as directed.

MILD CHOCOLATE COOKIE VARIATION: Add 1 ounce (1 square) *grated* Baker's All Natural Unsweetened Chocolate to the date sugar mixture in step 3. Continue as directed.

Cashew Butter or Peanut Butter Cookies

½ cup vegetable shortening or lard

2 teaspoons vegetable oil

½ cup cashew butter or peanut butter
(all-natural, unsweetened; if using
cashew butter, add an additional ½
teaspoon oil)

1 cup date sugar

2 egg whites or 1 extralarge egg, beaten

¼ cup plus 1 tablespoon water

1¼ cups all-purpose flour

¼ teaspoon salt

1¼ teaspoons baking soda

½ teaspoon baking powder

1. Preheat oven to 350°F. Grease two cookie sheets with vegetable shortening or oil.

2. In a large bowl, combine all ingredients except baking soda and baking powder and beat well by hand.

3. Add baking soda and baking powder and mix quickly but well.

4. Quickly form mixture into about 30 small balls, place on prepared cookie sheets, and flatten slightly with a fork.

5. Bake 10 to 12 minutes, or until cookies are slightly golden around edges. Rotate cookie sheets at the halfway point to achieve even baking. Remove cookie sheets from oven, remove cookies from sheets, and place on a countertop to cool. To store, place cooled cookies in an airtight container and store on countertop or freeze.

Yield: 30 cookies

PER COOKIE

Calories: 94

Protein: 1.6 g

Fat: 6.0 g

Carbohydrate: 8.2 g

Sodium: 59.8 mg

Diabetic exchanges

   Starch: ½

   Fat: 1¼

Rice Circle Cookies (Shortening-Based)

Gluten-Free

¾ cup vegetable shortening
¾ cup brown-rice syrup (Sweet
  Dreams Premium Brown-Rice
  Syrup by Lundberg; make sure label
  states "Gluten-Free")
4 egg whites or 2 extralarge eggs
1 teaspoon vanilla

2¼ cups brown-rice flour, tapped
  lightly 4 to 5 times
1¾ teaspoons Featherweight Baking
  Powder
1 teaspoon salt
Additional brown-rice flour for patting
  out dough

1. In a large bowl, cream together well shortening and brown-rice syrup. Add eggs and vanilla and mix together well.

2. In a medium-sized bowl, stir together brown-rice flour, baking powder, and salt, using a large wooden spoon. Add flour mixture to shortening mixture slowly, stirring ingredients well.

3. Chill cookie dough *uncovered* for 1½ hours in the refrigerator.

4. Preheat oven to 325°F. Grease two cookie sheets with oil. You will also need a large glass or large circle cookie cutter and a spatula.

5. Spread a small portion of additional brown-rice flour over a small section of counter surface. Take a small portion of dough at a time and knead in a little flour to make dough less sticky. Sprinkle surface with brown-rice flour again and pat dough out to ¼-inch thickness. Cut into circles using a large glass or large circle cookie cutters. Use a spatula to transfer cookies to prepared cookie sheets. Repeat procedure until all dough is used.

6. Bake 10 to 11 minutes, or until cookies look dry and have just a hint of gold on bottoms. Rotate cookie sheets at halfway point to achieve even baking.

7. Remove pans from oven; remove cookies from pans and place on countertop until completely cool. Store in an airtight container in refrigerator or freeze.

Yield: 21 to 25 cookies

PER COOKIE

Calories: 153
Protein: 1.9 g
Fat: 7.8 g
Carbohydrate: 18.9 g

Sodium: 114 mg
Diabetic exchanges
  Starch: 1
  Fat: 1½

VARIATION: For holidays, dough can be cut out with various cookie cutter shapes, such as christmas trees, stars, hearts, rabbits, or Easter eggs.

Rice Circle Cookies (Oil-Based)

Gluten-Free

½ cup vegetable oil
¾ cup brown-rice syrup (Sweet
　Dreams Premium Brown Rice
　Syrup by Lundberg; make sure label
　states "Gluten-Free")
4 egg whites or 2 extralarge eggs
1 teaspoon vanilla

2½ cups brown-rice flour, tapped well
　4 to 5 times
1¾ teaspoons Featherweight Baking
　Powder
1 teaspoon salt
Additional brown-rice flour for patting
　out dough

1. In a blender, place oil, brown-rice syrup, eggs, and vanilla. Blend ingredients on high for a minute, or until mixture resembles a rich syrup.

2. In a large-sized bowl, stir together brown-rice flour, baking powder, and salt, using a large wooden spoon. Add syrup mixture to flour mixture, scraping sides of blender to get out all the syrup. Stir well.

3. Chill cookie dough *uncovered* for 1 ½ hours in refrigerator.

4. Preheat oven to 325°F. Grease two cookie sheets with oil. You will also need a large glass or large circle cookie cutter and a spatula.

5. Spread a small portion of additional brown-rice flour over a small section of counter surface. Take a small portion of dough at a time and knead in a little extra flour to make dough less sticky. Sprinkle surface with brown-rice flour again and pat dough out to ¼-inch thickness. Cut into circles using a large glass or large circle cookie cutter. Use a spatula to transfer cookies to prepared cookie sheets. Repeat procedure until all dough is used.

6. Bake 11 to 13 minutes, or until cookies look dry and have just a hint of gold on bottoms. Rotate cookie sheets at halfway point to achieve even baking.

7. Remove pans from oven; remove cookies from pans and place on countertop until completely cool. Store in an airtight container in refrigerator or freeze.

Yield: 21 to 25 cookies

PER COOKIE

Calories: 141	*Sodium:* 114 mg
Protein: 2.0 g	*Diabetic exchanges*
Fat: 5.7 g	*Starch:* 1
Carbohydrate: 20.4 g	*Fat:* 1

VARIATION: For holidays, dough can be cut out with various cookie cutter shapes, such as christmas trees, stars, hearts, rabbits, or Easter eggs.

Fruity-Nut Cookies

Generous ½ cup chopped (cut with scissors) and packed dried Calimyrna figs

⅓ cup minced raisins, packed

Generous ⅓ cup minced dried diced pineapple

Generous ⅓ cup minced dried diced papaya

Generous ¼ cup chopped walnuts

½ cup unsweetened orange juice concentrate (Minute Maid Reduced Acid)

¾ cup unsweetened apple juice concentrate (any brand)

4 egg whites or 2 extralarge eggs

⅓ cup vegetable oil

1¼ teaspoons cinnamon

2½ cups plus 2 tablespoons all-purpose flour

2 teaspoons baking soda

1. Preheat oven to 350°F. Oil two or three large cookie sheets. Using scissors, chop figs; using a knife, mince raisins, pineapple, and papaya. Set aside. Chop nuts and set aside.

2. In a large bowl, stir together concentrates, figs, raisins, pineapple, papaya, eggs, oil, cinnamon, and nuts.

3. Add flour and mix well.

4. Add baking soda and mix quickly but well.

5. Quickly drop batter by tablespoonfuls onto prepared cookie sheets.

6. Bake 8 to 9 minutes, or until cookies are *slightly golden* and firm. Rotate cookie sheets at the halfway point to achieve even baking.

7. Remove pans from oven; remove cookies from pans and place on countertop until completely cool. To store, place cookies in an airtight container and store on countertop or freeze.

Yield: 39 to 40 cookies

PER COOKIE

Calories: 89
Protein: 1.5 g
Fat: 2.5 g
Carbohydrate: 15.5 g

Sodium: 76 mg
Diabetic exchanges
  Starch: 1
  Fat: ½

Graham-Cracker Cookie Cutouts

These cookies can be cut into any desired shape.

¾ cup vegetable shortening
1¼ cups date sugar
¼ cup water
4 egg whites *or* 2 extralarge eggs
2 tablespoons unsweetened apple juice concentrate (any brand)

2¾ cups all-purpose flour
½ teaspoon salt
1¼ teaspoons baking soda
¾ teaspoon baking powder
Chocolate-Date Frosting (page 55)

1. Preheat oven to 350°F. Oil two large cookie sheets.

2. In a large bowl, combine shortening, date sugar, and water and beat by hand until fluffy.

3. Add eggs and apple juice concentrate and stir well.

4. In a medium-sized bowl, combine flour, salt, baking soda, and baking powder, and stir until well mixed.

5. Gradually add flour mixture to shortening mixture, stirring well after each addition.

6. Place dough on a lightly floured surface and roll out to ¼-inch thickness. Cut into cookie shapes using cookie cutters. Place cut-out dough on prepared cookie sheets.

7. Bake 11 to 12 minutes, or until cookies are golden around edges. Rotate cookie sheets at halfway point to achieve even baking.

8. Remove pans from oven; remove cookies from pans and place on countertop until completely cool.

9. Spread Chocolate-Date Frosting on cooled cookies. Allow frosting to dry before serving or storing in an airtight container on countertop or freezer.

Yield: 18 cookies

PER COOKIE (WITHOUT FROSTING)

Calories: 185
Protein: 2.8 g
Fat: 8.7 g
Carbohydrate: 23.8 g

Sodium: 180 mg
Diabetic exchanges
  Starch: 1½
  Fat: 2

Oatmeal/Coconut-Date Cookies

¾ cup date sugar

5 tablespoons vegetable oil

2 egg whites *or* 1 extralarge egg

¼ cup water

Generous 1½ cups rolled oats

½ cup all-purpose flour

½ teaspoon salt

¼ cup unsweetened coconut, premoistened with 1 teaspoon water and 1 teaspoon vegetable oil

⅓ cup chopped (cut with scissors) and packed dried figs, premixed with 1½ teaspoons all-purpose flour

⅓ cup packed raisins

½ cup chopped (cut with scissors) and packed dates, premixed with 1½ teaspoons all-purpose flour

1 teaspoon baking soda

1. Preheat oven to 325°F. Oil two large cookie sheets.

2. In a medium sized bowl, beat together date sugar, oil, egg, and water.

3. In a large bowl, stir together oats, flour, salt, coconut, figs, raisins, dates, and baking soda.

4. Pour oat mixture a little at a time into egg-and-water mixture and stir well.

5. Quickly drop batter by tablespoonfuls on prepared cookie sheets. Flatten cookies slightly with a fork.

6. Bake 13 to 14 minutes, or until cookies are slightly golden around edges. Rotate cookie sheets at the halfway point to achieve even baking.

7. Remove pans from oven; remove cookies from pans and place on countertop until completely cool. To store, place cooled cookies in an airtight container and refrigerate or freeze.

Yield: 28 cookies

PER COOKIE

Calories: 82

Protein: 1.6 g

Fat: 3.3 g

Carbohydrate: 12.6 g

Sodium: 68.5 mg

Diabetic exchanges

Starch: ½

Fat: ½

Fruit: ½

Crispy Rice-Date Bars (or Caramel ''Popcorn'')

4 rice cakes, crumbled (use any brand; omit additional salt if using salted rice cakes)
Scant ¼ teaspoon sea salt
Generous ¼ teaspoon allspice
13 finely chopped (cut with scissors) dates

3 tablespoons plus 1½ teaspoons brown-rice syrup (Sweet Dreams Brown Rice Syrup by Lundberg, make sure label states ''Gluten-Free'')

1. Preheat oven to 300°F. Oil a 9- by 9- by 2-inch baking pan.
2. In a large bowl, stir together all ingredients except rice syrup.
3. Add rice syrup 1 tablespoon at a time, stirring well after each addition.
4. Pour mixture into prepared baking pan. Dampen hands with water and press mixture firmly into pan.
5. Bake 15 minutes, or until bars feel dry and not sticky to the touch.
6. Remove pan from oven and place on a wire rack to cool for 15 to 18 minutes. With a down-up motion, use a spatula to cut into 9 bars. Remove bars from pan and place in an airtight container. Leave in bar shape or break into small pieces to serve as caramel ''popcorn.'' Do not refrigerate.

Yield: 9 bars

PER BAR

Calories: 64
Protein: 0.7 g
Fat: less than 0.1 g
Carbohydrate: 15.5 g
Sodium: 76.3 mg
Diabetic exchanges
  Starch: ½
  Fruit: ½

COLD
FRESH FRUIT
DRINKS
AND
SORBETS

Nothing beats the taste of a cold fruit drink or fruit malt or fruit sorbet, especially in the summer. And a bowl of fresh fruit salad can be the perfect finishing touch to any special meal. Almost any fruit or combination of fruits will work. Just remember that for the best taste and appearance and for maximum vitamin content, you should choose fruit that is undamaged and at the height of ripeness.

Because of the many variables, it is difficult to provide useful nutritional analyses for the recipes in this chapter. The following charts should provide some guidance, however.

Nutritional Analysis of Fresh Fruit

Fresh Fruit	Calories	Protein (grams)	Fat (grams)	Carbohydrate (grams)	Sodium (milligrams)	Diabetic Exchanges
Apple (1 medium)	81	0.3	0.5	21.0	1.0	Fruit: 1⅓
Apricot (3 medium)	51	1.5	0.4	11.8	1.0	Fruit: 1
Banana, mashed (per cup)	207	2.3	1.1	52.7	2.0	Fruit: 3½
Blueberries (per cup)	82	1.0	0.6	20.5	9.0	Fruit: 1⅓
Cantaloupe (½ of 5-inch-diameter fruit)	80	2.5	0.7	18.0	23.1	Fruit: 1⅓

Fresh Fruit	Calories	Protein (grams)	Fat (grams)	Carbohydrate (grams)	Sodium (milligrams)	Diabetic Exchanges
Cherries, sweet (20 cherries)	98	1.6	1.3	22.5	0.9	Fruit: 1½
Grapefruit (½ medium)	39	0.8	0.1	9.9	0	Fruit: ½
Grapes (per cup)	114	1.1	0.9	28.4	3.0	Fruit: 2
Honeydew (2- × 7-inch slice)	46	0.6	0.1	11.8	12.9	Fruit: ¾
Kiwi (2 fruit)	92	1.5	0.7	22.6	8.0	Fruit: 1½
Mango (1 medium)	135	1.1	0.6	35.2	3.8	Fruit: 2¼
Nectarine (1 medium)	67	1.3	0.6	16.0	0	Fruit: 1
Orange (1 medium)	62	1.2	0.2	15.4	0	Fruit: 1
Papaya (1 medium)	117	1.9	0.4	29.8	8.0	Fruit: 2
Peach (per cup)	73	1.2	0.2	18.9	1.0	Fruit: 1¼
Pear (1 medium)	98	0.7	0.7	25.1	1.0	Fruit: 1½
Plum (3 medium)	119	1.7	1.4	28.3	0	Fruit: 2
Raspberries (per cup)	61	1.1	0.7	14.2	0	Fruit: 1
Strawberries (per cup)	45	0.9	0.6	10.5	2.0	Fruit: ¾
Watermelon (per cup)	50	1.0	0.7	11.5	3.0	Fruit: ¾

Nutritional Analysis of Fruit Juices

Fresh Fruit	Calories	Protein (grams)	Fat (grams)	Carbohydrate (grams)	Sodium (milligrams)	Diabetic Exchanges
Apple (per cup)	116	0.2	0.3	29.0	5.0	Fruit: 2
Apricot nectar (per cup)	120	0.7	0.2	30.0	0	Fruit: 2
Grape (per cup)	155	1.4	0.2	37.9	8.0	Fruit: 2½
Grapefruit (per cup)	96	1.2	0.3	22.7	2.0	Fruit: 1½
Lemon (per tablespoon)	4	0.1	0	1.3	0.1	Free
Orange (per cup)	111	1.7	0.5	25.8	2.0	Fruit: 2
Peach nectar (per cup)	100	0.5	0	25.0	2.0	Fruit: 1⅔
Pear nectar (per cup)	110	0.7	0.5	28.0	2.0	Fruit: 2
Pineapple (per cup)	139	0.8	0.2	34.4	5.0	Fruit: 2¼
Prune (per cup)	181	1.6	0.1	44.6	5.0	Fruit: 3

Nutritional Analysis of Frozen Fruit Juice Concentrates

(Data is based on 1 cup—8 ounces—of the actual concentrate, unsweetened and undiluted with water.)

Frozen Fruit Juice Concentrate	Calories	Protein (grams)	Fat (grams)	Carbohydrate (grams)	Sodium (milligrams)	Diabetic Exchanges
Apple-Minute Maid	485	0.6	1.1	120.8	121.7	Fruit: 8
Orange (Reduced Acid) Minute Maid	475	7.4	0.6	116.6	101.4	Fruit: 7¾
White Grape-Welch's	680	0	0	168	80	Fruit: 11
Purple Grape-Welch's	640	0	0	164	0	Fruit: 11

Nutritional Analysis of Non-Frozen Fruit Juice Concentrates

Black Cherry-Tree of Life R. W. Knudsen	779	0	0	180	60	Fruit: 12

Fruit Frappe

1 cup unsweetened fruit (peach, pear,
   berries, banana)
4 ice cubes

Place fruit and ice cubes in a blender and blend to desired consistency.

Yield: 1 serving

Fruit Soda

½ cup unsweetened fruit juice of
   choice or combination of juices
½ cup sparkling mineral water
Lemon or lime slice (optional)

Combine juice and mineral water. If desired, garnish with lemon or lime.

Yield: 1 serving

Peach Shake

2 cups peeled, pitted, and sliced
   peaches
1/4 cup cold water

Place peaches and water in a blender and blend to desired consistency.

Yield: 2 servings

Banana Shake

1 banana, peeled and sliced
1 cup cold water

Place banana and water in a blender and blend to desired consistency.

Yield: 1 serving

Fruit Sherbet

1 cup partially thawed frozen fruit

Place fruit in a blender or food processor and blend until the fruit is the consistency of sherbet. Serve immediately.

Yield: 1 serving

Orange Sherbet

½ cup unsweetened apple juice
   concentrate (any brand)
⅓ cup unsweetened orange juice
   concentrate (Minute Maid
   Reduced Acid)

¾ cup plus 2 tablespoons water
1 tablespoon olive oil

1. In a medium-sized mixing bowl, combine all ingredients and beat with an electric mixer for 30 seconds every 30 to 45 minutes for a period of 3 to 3½ hours. Between beatings, place mixture in freezer.

2. Ten minutes before serving, remove mixture from freezer. Let it sit for 5 to 10 minutes at room temperature, then beat with mixer for 30 seconds and serve.

Yield: 2 servings

Fresh Fruit Ice Cream

1 frozen banana (to freeze, place
   unpeeled ripe banana in airtight
   plastic bag in freezer)

1 to 2 tablespoons chopped fruit of your
   choice
½ tablespoon chopped nuts (optional)

Remove banana from freezer and thaw for ½ hour. Peel and mash partially thawed banana with a fork. Add chopped fruit and nuts and stir. Serve immediately.

Yield: 1 serving

Raspberry Popsicles

¼ cup water
10 raspberries (red)
1 peach or nectarine, peeled, pitted,
  and sliced
4 to 5 ice cubes

Place water, fruit, and one ice cube in a blender and blend, adding one ice cube at a time, until mixture is the consistency of slush. Pour into plastic molds, adding popsicle sticks if desired, to make real popsicles. Freeze.

Yield: 6 servings

Fresh Fruit Bowl

1 banana, peeled, cut into slices, and
  dipped in orange juice
1 apple, peeled, cored, sliced, and
  dipped in orange juice
1 orange, peeled and sliced
1 peach, peeled, pitted, sliced, and
  dipped in orange juice
10 strawberries, hulled and sliced

10 seedless grapes, white and/or red
4 kiwis, peeled and sliced
½ cantaloupe, with rind and seeds
  removed, cut into slices
¼ honeydew melon, with rind and
  seeds removed, cut into slices
1 cup watermelon, with rind removed,
  cut into slices

Combine all fruits in a large bowl or in half of a scooped-out watermelon. Refrigerate, covered, until ready to serve.

Yield: 8 servings

Summer Afternoon Malt

4 to 5 ice cubes
3 tablespoons water
8 pitted dark sweet cherries

2 peeled, pitted, and sliced nectarines
2 peeled, pitted, and sliced apricots
2 peeled, pitted, and sliced plums

Place ice cubes, water, and fruit in a blender and blend to desired consistency.

Yield: 2 servings

Blueberry, Raspberry, Strawberry Malt

1 to 2 cups strawberries, semi-frozen
1 to 2 cups blueberries, semi-frozen
1 to 2 cups raspberries, semi-frozen
 (red or black)

6 tablespoons (3 ounces) unsweetened
 apple juice concentrate (any brand)

Place fruits and concentrate in a blender and blend to desired consistency.

Yield: 2 to 3 servings

Malt Shop Surprise

5 to 6 ice cubes
1 large or 2 small peeled, pitted, and
 sliced plums
1 large or 2 small peeled, pitted, and
 sliced nectarines or peaches

¾ cup (6 ounces) unsweetened apple
 juice concentrate (any brand)

Place ice cubes, fruit and concentrate in a blender and blend to desired consistency.

Yield: 2 servings

Fresh Fruit Delight

¾ cup seedless green and red grapes
½ cup sliced, fresh strawberries
½ cup fresh red raspberries
½ cup unsweetened pineapple chunks, drained

8 tablespoons unsweetened apple juice concentrate (any brand), or 4 tablespoons apple juice concentrate (any brand) plus 4 tablespoons unsweetened orange juice concentrate (Minute Maid Reduced Acid), partially thawed and mashed with a fork

Toss fruit gently and divide among four dessert dishes. Just before serving, place 2 tablespoons mashed concentrate on top of fruit in each dish. Serve cold immediately.

Yield: 4 servings

EXTRAS

Including Dips,
Dressings, Salads,
and Potato
Substitutes

The recipes in this section are for those of you with food sensitivities looking for a little something extra. They add fun to any meal, and some are great as a snack instead of a piece of cake or pie.

Toasting nuts and seeds makes them more flavorful. They go with any meal, and toasted pumpkin seeds are especially great for eating out of hand. For those of you who might dislike or can't have commercial peanut butter, there's nothing like homemade nut butter spread on freshly baked bread. Making it yourself allows *you* to control the freshness of the ingredients and the type and amount of oil.

The mayonnaise and dips add excitement to lettuce salads and finger vegetables. They make vegetables a lot more interesting and flavorful. And the potato salads? Let me just say that sometimes my daughter will ask for another helping of potato salad instead of a piece of cake or pie for dessert. Now that's a compliment!

For those who are allergic to potatoes—or are just tired of them—I have included information about potato alternatives and other starch substitutes in this section. It gives a little variety to the dinner table. Each potato alternative has a different flavor and texture, but I find them all quite enjoyable. I've used ñame and Malanga to make potato salad and really could not tell the difference. Check the sources section (page 205) for information on where and how to obtain these potato substitutes.

BONIATO

This white sweet potato is a member of the morning glory family. It is moderately high in calories at 115 calories per ½ cup. Boniato is a staple through Asia and Mexico and tastes like a cross between a sweet potato and a baking potato. The skin may be pinkish, purplish, or reddish. You can do anything with boniato that you can do with any common American sweet potato. *Do not eat raw.*

To prepare, peel boniato and place in cold water so the flesh will not discolor. Cut into medium-sized pieces and boil in salted water about 25 minutes, or until tender when tested with a fork. Drain and serve whole or drain and add a little of the cooking liquid and mash for mashed boniato.

JÍCAMA (pronounced HEE-ka-mah)

Jícama, a member of the legume family, is a fleshy underground tuber grown in Asia and Mexico. It's shaped like a turnip and has a sandy-tan skin. It's low in calories with only 50 calories per cup (raw). It's also low in sodium and a good diet food. Jícama is crunchy and juicy with ivory flesh the texture of water chestnuts. It has a sweet and bland flavor. *It can be eaten raw or cooked.*

To prepare, peel the jícama, and cut into sticks, slices, or dice. Use with vegetable dips, diced in salads or soups, stir-fried, or in place of water chestnuts.

MALANGA

The forty or so species are all native to the American tropics. They are a member of the arum family, *Xanthosoma* species. Malanga is high in calories, 135 calories per ½ cup. It's long in shape and firm, shaggy and brown in appearance. Its flesh is cream or pinkish, and is crisp and slippery. The taste is quite pronounced, a cross between cooked dried pinto beans and a potato. It blends well with stews, soups, meats, and other root vegetables. Makes a good potato substitute. *Do not eat raw.*

To prepare, pare with a knife to remove skin and imperfections, rinse, and place in cold water to keep from discoloring. Cut into medium-sized chunks, cover with salted water, and boil until just tender, 20 to 25 minutes. Or shred and pan-fry with a little oil like hash brown potatoes.

ÑAME (pronounced nyAH-may)

Ñame is a member of the yam family. Yams are produced by most countries in the tropics and subtropics. They are brown, shaggy-coated tubers. Yams provide an excellent supply of potassium and zinc and are moderate in calories, with 80 calories per cup. Their flesh is crisp, slippery, and either white or off-white. A cooked yam's taste will be similar to a potato, but the texture will be loose, coarser, and drier. They are boiled like potatoes, cooked in stews, or pan-fried. *Do not eat raw.*

To prepare, peel, cut into chunks, rinse, and place in a bowl of water so the flesh will not discolor. Drop into boiling salted water and gently simmer until just tender when pierced with a fork, 30 to 40 minutes. Or shred and pan-fry flesh in a little oil like hash brown potatoes.

TARO

Taro, also know as yantia and poi, is an edible tropical tuber in the arum family. It is grown in California, Hawaii, Brazil, and Costa Rica. It is about the size of a little new potato, is elongated in size with a smooth form, and is quite ''hairy'' with distinct rings. It is moderate in calories at 100 calories per ½ cup and is an excellent source of potassium and a fairly good source of fiber. It is very low in sodium. The flesh is smooth, white to cream or lilac-gray. The taste and texture are like a combination of water chestnuts and potatoes. Boiled taro can be used in soups and stews, or shredded and pan-fried. *Do not eat raw.*

To prepare, peel and remove discolored spots. Immediately place in cold water. Boil covered, until tender, 25 to 40 minutes depending on size of pieces. The flesh will turn to a drab grayish or purplish color. Test with a fork for tenderness. Serve hot. Or shred and pan-fry in a little oil like hash brown potatoes.

YUCA (pronounced YOO-ka)

Yuca is a member of the spurge family (tapioca). It's cultivated in South and Central America and Florida. Yuca is long, narrow, firm, and covered with bark. It is high in calories at 135 calories per ½ cup. It is a good source of iron, and has small amounts of niacin and calcium. Underneath the brown bark is hard, dense white flesh, which becomes almost translucent when cooked and has a sweet and buttery flavor. When used in soups, stews, and boiled, yuca becomes sticky and thickens and absorbs liquids. *Do not eat raw.*

To prepare, trim and slice off bark. Lay yuca on its side and cut into 2-inch chunks, lay each chunk on flat cut side, and cut into 2 to 4 pieces. Discard the central fibrous cord that runs down the middle of the yuca. Rinse and place in cold water. Simmer yuca in plenty of salted water for 20 to 30 minutes. Test for doneness using a fork. Do not undercook or cook to a mush; it should be tender. Drain and serve hot. Or shred and pan-fry in a little oil like hash brown potatoes.

Nutritional Analysis of Nuts

Ingredient	Measure	Calories	Protein g	Carbohydrate g	Sodium mg	Cholesterol mg g	Saturated g	Unsaturated g	Lipid g
Coconut, shredded	1 cup	277	2.8	7.5	18	0	24.3	2	28.2
Pumpkin seeds	1 cup	774	40.6	21	24	0	11.8	51	65.4
Almonds	1 cup	849	26.4	27.7	6	0	6.2	67	77
Cashews	1 cup	785	24.1	41	21	0	10.9	49.3	64
Hazelnut	1 cup	856	17	22.5	3	0	4.2	59	84.2
Peanuts	1 cup	838	37.7	29.7	7	0	15.4	50.5	70.1
Peanut butter	1 Tablespoon	86	3.9	3.2	18	0	1.5	6.1	8.1
Pecans	1 cup	742	9.9	15.8	t	0	5.4	63.8	76.9
Pine nuts	1 ounce	180	3.7	5.8	1	0	1.7	11.7	14.3
Sesame seeds	1 cup	873	27.3	26.4	59	0	11.2	64	80
Sunflower seeds	1 cup	812	34.8	28.9	4	0	8.2	56.9	68.6
Walnuts	1 cup	651	14.8	15.8	2	0	4.5	49.5	64

Nutrition Almanac, Third Edition by Lavon J. Dunne, McGraw-Hill Publishing Company, Section VII, Table of Food Composition, page 293.

Sesame Salad Dressing

Make 1 hour before serving.

¼ cup sesame oil
2 tablespoons freshly squeezed lemon
   juice
⅛ teaspoon salt
Generous ⅛ teaspoon black pepper

⅛ teaspoon sesame seeds
¼ teaspoon celery flakes
Generous ½ teaspoon dried dillweed
¼ teaspoon fennel seeds
¼ teaspoon caraway seeds

1. Place all ingredients in a glass jar. Stir well. Set aside for an hour to let flavors combine.

2. Stir well before using. Use on lettuce salads as a salad dressing or use as a dip for crudités.

Yield: 2 servings

PER SERVING

Calories: 248
Protein: 0.2 g
Fat: 27.5 g
Carbohydrate: 1.9 g

Sodium: 129 mg
Diabetic exchanges
  Fat: 5½

VARIATION. Try different spice combinations such as dry mustard, parsley, paprika, curry powder, garlic powder, or onion powder.

Salad Dressing with Olive Oil

Make at least one hour before using.

2 tablespoons extra-light, mild-tasting olive oil

2 tablespoons extra-virgin or full-bodied olive oil

2 tablespoons freshly squeezed lemon juice

Generous ⅛ teaspoon salt

Generous ⅛ teaspoon black pepper

Generous ½ teaspoon dried dillweed or dried parsley flakes

¼ teaspoon fennel seeds

¼ teaspoon caraway seeds

⅛ teaspoon celery seeds

¼ teaspoon celery flakes

1. Place all ingredients in a jar. Stir ingredients well to mix. Set aside for an hour to let flavors combine.

2. Stir well before using. Use on lettuce salads as a dressing or use as a dip for crudités.

Yield: 2 servings

PER SERVING

Calories: 246
Protein: 0.2 g
Fat: 27.1 g
Carbohydrate: 1.9 g

Sodium: 129 mg
Diabetic exchanges
  Fat: 5½

VARIATION: Try different spice combinations such as dry mustard, paprika, curry powder, garlic powder, or onion powder.

Almond Salad Dressing

Make one hour before serving.

¼ cup almond oil

Scant 2 tablespoons to 2 tablespoons
freshly squeezed lime juice

Generous ⅛ teaspoon salt

Generous ⅛ teaspoon black pepper

Generous ½ teaspoon dried dillweed or
parsley

Generous ⅛ teaspoon celery seeds

⅛ teaspoon poppy seeds

¼ teaspoon fennel seeds

¼ teaspoon caraway seeds

¼ teaspoon celery flakes

1. Place all ingredients in a glass jar. Stir well. Set aside for an hour to let flavors combine.

2. Stir well before using. Use on lettuce salads as a salad dressing or as a dip for crudités.

Yield: 2 servings

PER SERVING

Calories. 249
Protein: 0.3 g
Fat: 27.5 g
Carbohydrate: 2.0 g

Sodium: 129 mg
Diabetic exchanges
Fat: 5½

VARIATION: Try different spice combinations using dry mustard, paprika, curry powder, garlic powder, onion powder or sesame seeds.

Quick Lettuce Salad Dressing

Make at least one hour before using.

¼ cup extra-light, mild-tasting olive oil   2 tablespoons lemon juice
Ground black pepper to taste   Generous ½ teaspoon dried dillweed
Salt to taste

1. Place all ingredients in a jar. Stir well to mix. Set aside for an hour to let flavors combine.
2. Stir well before using. Use on lettuce salads as a salad dressing or as a dip for crudités.

Yield: 2 servings

PER SERVING

Calories: 243   *Sodium:* 129 mg
Protein: 0.1 g   *Diabetic exchanges*
Fat: 27 g   *Fat:* 5½
Carbohydrate: 1.6 g

Lobster or Orange Ruffy Dip

¼ cup pure virgin or Classico olive oil
Ground black pepper to taste
Salt to taste

2 tablespoons plus 1 teaspoon lemon juice

1. In a very small pan, combine oil, black pepper, salt, and lemon juice. Stir well to mix.

2. Heat on stove, stirring constantly, just before serving.

Yield: Enough dip for 3 lobsters

PER SERVING

Calories: 163
Protein: 0.1 g
Fat: 18 g
Carbohydrate: 1.1 g

Sodium: 85.3 mg
Diabetic exhanges
Fat: 3½

VARIATION: Place ingredients in a small dish and stir well. Serve cold with cold ''popcorn'' shrimp.

Potato Salad

Contains Eggs—Not Cholesterol-Free

2½ cups peeled, cooked, and cubed
 cold potatoes
Generous ⅛ cup diced onion
¼ cup diced celery
¼ cup diced green pepper
¼ cup diced radish
Generous ⅛ cup chopped broccoli
Generous ⅛ cup chopped cauliflower
3 extralarge hard-boiled eggs, yolks
 divided

About ½ cup Non-dairy dillweed
 mayonnaise (see page 000)
Salt to taste
Black pepper to taste
Dry mustard to taste
Dried dillweed to taste

1. In a large mixing bowl, gently toss potatoes, onion, celery, green pepper, radish, broccoli, and cauliflower.

2. Using a knife, cut 2 hard-boiled eggs in half, pry out the egg yolks, and place 1½ yolks on a large plate. Using a fork, mash the egg yolks. Add mayonnaise to the egg yolks and mix well. Pour mayonnaise mixture over prepared vegetables.

3. Chop the remaining hard-boiled eggs and add to the potato salad. Toss ingredients lightly until dressing is evenly distributed. Add salt, pepper, mustard, and dillweed to taste. Toss ingredients to mix well.

4. Refrigerate uneaten potato salad in an airtight container with a lid. Eat within 2 or 3 days.

Yield: 4 servings

PER SERVING

Calories: 324
Protein: 8.9 g
Fat: 22.5 g
Carbohydrate: 22.5 g

Sodium: 329 mg
Diabetic exchanges
 Starch: 1½
 Fat: 4½
 Lean Meat: 1

VARIATION: Try adding chunk light tuna, packed in water with no salt added.

Egg-Free Potato Salad

About 1 cup egg-free mayonnaise (see
  page 000)
1 teaspoon dry mustard
1½ teaspoons lemon juice
5 cups peeled, cooked, and cubed cold
  potatoes
⅛ cup to ¼ cup diced onion, optional
⅛ cup to ⅓ cup diced celery

⅛ cup to ⅓ cup diced green pepper
⅛ cup to ⅓ cup diced radish
⅛ cup to ¼ cup chopped broccoli
⅛ cup to ¼ cup chopped cauliflower
Dried dillweed to taste
Salt and pepper to taste
Lemon juice to taste

1. In a small bowl, combine egg-free mayonnaise, mustard, and lemon juice.

2. In a large mixing bowl, gently stir potatoes, onion, celery, green pepper, radish, broccoli, and cauliflower. Add mayonnaise mixture. Toss ingredients lightly until dressing is evenly distributed. Add dillweed, salt and pepper, and lemon juice to taste. Toss ingredients to mix well.

3. Refrigerate potato salad in an airtight container with lid. Use within 2 days.

Yield: 8 servings

PER SERVING

Calories: 177
Protein: 2.1 g
Fat: 9.1 g
Carbohydrate. 21.8 g

Sodium: 128 mg
Diabetic exchanges
  Starch: 1½
  Fat: 2

Note: You can use different proportions of vegetables to potatoes, or try different vegetables—according to your taste.

Nondairy Dillweed Dip or Mayonnaise

This dip is great with fresh vegetables such as peppers, broccoli, cauliflower, carrots, celery, and on lettuce. It also goes well with grapes and chopped apples. Make at least four hours ahead of use so dip can chill and thicken.

2 egg whites or 1 extralarge egg
Generous 1 tablespoon lemon juice
½ cup extra-light, mild-tasting olive oil
¼ teaspoon salt

¼ teaspoon black pepper
¼ teaspoon dry mustard
Generous 1 teaspoon dried dillweed, or
   to taste

1. In a small deep bowl, whip ingredients with an electric mixer or hand blender (or place ingredients in a blender and blend on high) until creamy.
2. Place in a container. Cover and refrigerate. Use within 3 days or freeze.

Yield: About ¾ cup dip or mayonnaise (6 servings)

PER SERVING

Calories: 166
Protein: 1.2 g
Fat: 18.0 g
Carbohydrate: 0.5 g

Sodium: 196 mg
Diabetic exchanges
   Fat: 3½

VARIATION: Omit dillweed and try different spice combinations—paprika, curry powder, garlic, onion salt, parsley, or other spices or seeds.

Egg-Free Dillweed Dip or Mayonnaise

This dip can be used on peppers, broccoli, lettuce, cauliflower, or any fresh vegetable. Try it on chopped apples or grapes. Make at least four hours ahead of use.

2 tablespoons potato starch flour, rice flour, cornstarch, or arrowroot (see *Note*)
½ teaspoon salt
¼ teaspoon dry mustard
1 cup water, divided into ¼ cup and ¾ cup

Generous 1 teaspoon to generous 2 teaspoons dried dillweed, or to taste
1 tablespoon plus ½ to 1 teaspoon lemon juice
½ cup extra-light, mild-tasting olive oil

1. In a medium-sized saucepan, combine flour, salt, mustard, and ¼ cup water. Stir until smooth. Add the rest of the water and cook over medium heat, stirring constantly, until mixture thickens and comes to a boil. Remove from heat. Let mixture cool to lukewarm.

2. Place cooled mixture in a blender. Add dillweed. In a small bowl, combine lemon juice and oil; stir to mix. With the blender on *low* speed, add the oil mixture, scraping bowl well. Oil should "dissolve" and mixture should be all white in color. Overblending tends to thin the consistency; not blending enough tends to make it too thick.

3. Pour dip into an airtight container with lid and store in refrigerator. If mixture becomes too thick, stir before using. Use within 2 or 3 days.

Yield. About 1½ cups vegetable dip or mayonnaise (12 servings)

PER SERVING
Calories: 86
Fat: 9.0 g
Carbohydrate: 1.6 g
Sodium: 89.6 mg
Diabetic exchanges
 Fat: 2

Note: For information on how to use arrowroot and cornstarch, see page 00.

VARIATION: Omit dillweed and try different spice combinations—paprika, curry powder, garlic, onion salt, parsley, or other spices or seeds.

Light Dillweed Dip

No Dairy, Egg, or Oil

This dip can be used on peppers, broccoli, lettuce, cauliflower, or any fresh vegetable. I even like having it with some fresh fruit, such as grapes or chopped apple. Make at least four hours before use.

2 generous tablespoons potato starch flour or cornstarch (see *Note*)	Generous 1¼ cups water
½ teaspoon salt	3 generous tablespoons lemon juice
¼ teaspoon dry mustard	1½ tablespoons dried dillweed
	Generous ¼ cup water

1. In a medium-sized saucepan over medium heat, cook the potato starch flour, salt, mustard, and 1¼ cups water, stirring constantly, until mixture thickens and comes to a boil.

2. Remove saucepan from heat. Add lemon juice, dillweed, and generous ¼ cup water to hot mixture. Depending on the desired consistency, you can add ¼ teaspoon to 1 teaspoon more water if you wish. Stir ingredients together well.

3. Pour vegetable dip into an airtight container with lid and refrigerate. If mixture becomes too thick, stir before using. Use within a day or two.

Yield: About 1½ cups vegetable dip (12 servings)

PER SERVING

Calories: 8   *Carbohydrate:* 2.0 g
Protein: 0.1 g   *Sodium:* 90.3 mg

Note: For information on how to use cornstarch, see page 136.

VARIATION: Omit dillweed and try different spice combinations—paprika, curry powder, garlic, onion salt, parsley, or other spices or seeds.

Nut Butter

You can use either raw or toasted nuts, but toasted nuts make more flavorful nut butters. Try peanuts, almonds, walnuts, cashews, or pecans. If you are using cashews, you might need to use more oil or water to get the desired consistency.

1 cup shelled raw or toasted nuts of
    choice

1 to 3 teaspoons vegetable oil or water
Salt to taste, optional

1. Using a food processor and on high speed, process nuts until they are ground fine.

2. Add oil or water a little at a time to the ground nuts and process to desired consistency. Add salt to taste, if you wish.

3. Place prepared nut butter in a container with a lid and refrigerate until ready to use.

Yield: About ¾ cup nut butter (6 servings)

PER SERVING (USING PEANUTS)

Calories: 149
Protein: 5.8 g
Fat: 13.0 g
Carbohydrate: 5.2 g
Sodium: 1.5 mg

Diabetic exchanges
  Fat: 2
  Fruit: ½
  Lean Meat: 1

Toasted Nuts

Try toasting walnuts, pecans, cashews, filberts, peanuts, or almonds. You can either dry-toast raw nuts or add a little oil before toasting.

1½ cups to 2 cups shelled raw nuts of choice	Few drops of vegetable oil, optional salt to taste, optional

1. Preheat oven to 250°F.

2. If you're using oil and salt, measure out raw nuts in a medium-sized bowl. Add oil and salt to taste. Stir.

3. Spread prepared raw nuts on a cookie sheet or jelly roll pan in a thin layer.

4. Bake 25 to 35 minutes, stirring nuts occasionally until they are fragrant and lightly tan in color. Do not overtoast or they might burn.

5. Take sheet out of oven and place on *protected* countertop surface so nuts can cool. Additional salt can be added, if you wish. To store, place cooled nuts in a plastic bag and refrigerate or freeze.

Yield: 1½ cups to 2 cups toasted nuts (12 to 16 servings)

PER SERVING (USING WALNUTS)

Calories: 96   *Sodium:* 1.5 mg
Protein: 2.2 g   *Diabetic exchanges*
Fat: 9.3 g   *Fat:* 2
Carbohydrate: 2.8 g

Toasted Sunflower Seeds

You can either dry-toast raw seeds or add a little oil to the seeds before toasting.

1½ cups shelled raw sunflower seeds
Few drops of vegetable oil, optional

Salt to taste, optional

1. Preheat oven to 250°F.

2. If you're using oil and salt, measure out raw seeds in a medium-sized bowl. Add oil and salt to taste. Stir.

3. Spread prepared raw seeds on a cookie sheet or jelly roll pan in a thin layer.

4. Bake 20 minutes or so, stirring seeds occasionally until they are fragrant and lightly tan in color. Do not overtoast or they might burn.

5. Take sheet out of oven and place on *protected* countertop surface so seeds can cool. Additional salt can be added, if you wish. To store, place cooled seeds in a plastic bag and refrigerate or freeze.

Yield: 1½ cups toasted sunflower seeds (12 servings)

PER SERVING (WITHOUT SALT)

Calories: 102
Protein: 4.1 g
Fat: 9.0 g
Carbohydrate: 3.4 g

Sodium: 0.5 mg
Diabetic exchanges
  Fat: 1½
  Lean Meat: ½

Panfried Pumpkin Seeds

2 teaspoons to 3 teaspoons vegetable oil   Salt to taste
¾ cup to 1 cup raw pumpkin seeds

1. Place paper towels on a large cookie sheet for draining panfried seeds.

2. In a large cold frying pan, place oil, pumpkin seeds, and salt. Using a spatula, mix together well. (You have enough oil on seeds for frying when the seeds are shiny and there is a hint of a layer of oil on pan's surface.)

3. On medium heat, panfry seeds, using a spatula to stir quite frequently to avoid burning them. Seeds will begin to "pop" like popcorn. Reduce temperature to low and, continuing to stir, fry until all seeds have popped, 10 to 12 minutes. The seeds will be medium in color, but not black.

4. Remove pan from stove. Using a spatula, remove seeds to prepared cookie sheet. Spread seeds out to drain excess oil. Sprinkle seeds with salt.

5. The seeds are good served warm or cold. To store, place cooled seeds in a plastic bag and refrigerate or freeze until ready to use.

Yield: ¾ cup to 1 cup panfried pumpkin seeds (4 to 5 servings)

PER SERVING (WITHOUT SALT)

Calories: 160   *Diabetic exchange*
Protein: 6.3 g   *Starch:* ½
Fat: 14.1 g   *Fat:* 2
Carbohydrate: 4.6 g   *Lean Meat:* 1
Sodium: 4.7 mg

SOURCES

- Where and how to get Potato Substitutes:
  Frieda, "The Specialty Produce People," supplies grocery stores all across
  the U.S. They carry many products including potato substitutes such
  as yuca, jícama, boniato, malanga, taro, and ñame.
  If you wish to try these products, simply ask the produce manager at
  your grocery store to order them for you. It usually takes two weeks
  to receive an order. Address: Frieda's, Inc., 4465 Corporate Center Drive,
  Los Alamilos, CA 90720-2561
- Products for the Environmentally Aware and Chemically Sensitive:
  Living Source Health and Home Store, P.O. Box 20155, Waco, TX
  76702. Telephone number: 1-817-776-4878.
  You can call Monday through Friday, 9A.M. to 5P.M. central time and
  request the *Source Book Catalogue*. The products they carry contain
  no perfumes, dyes, artificial colorings or agents, detergents, or
  preservatives, and include everything from bathroom supplies and cleaners
  to cosmetics, building supplies, and mattress and pillow covers.

INDEX

plums, nutritional analysis
  of, 175
potato flour, *xvi*
Potato Mix Waffles-Cereal-
  Free, 15
Potato Pizza Crust, 44-45
Potato Salad, 196
Potato Salad (Egg-Free), 197
potato substitutes, 186-87
  boniato, 186-87
  jícama, 187
  malanga, 187-88
  ñame, 188
  taro, 188-89
  where and how to get, 205
  yuca, 189
Prebaked Oil-Based Brown
  Rice Pie Crust, 93
Prebaked Rice Crumb-Crust
  Topping, 123
Prebaked Shortening-Based
  Brown Rice Pie Crust,
  92
preservatives, avoiding,
  xviii
prune juice, nutritional
  analysis of, 176
puddings
  Baked Apples, 145
  Quick Apple or Pear
    Pudding, 140
  Quick Peach Pudding, 144
  Raspberry Tapioca Pudding,
    138
  See also sauces
puddings (cooking)
  cooking time, 136
  stirring, 136
  thickeners, 136-37
  using covered saucepan,
    136
puddings (thickeners), 136-
  37
  arrowroot, 136
  cornstarch, 136
  equivalents, 137
  flour, 136

Minute Tapioca, 136-37
Pumpkin Pie, 108
pumpkin seeds
  nutritional analysis of,
    190
  toasted, 186
Pumpkin Seeds (Panfried), 204
Purity Foods Inc., *xvi, xix*

Q

Quick Apple or Pear Pudding,
  140
Quick Apple Upside-Down
  Cake, 77
Quick Brown Rice-Seed
  Topping, 123-24
Quick Lettuce Salad Dressing,
  194
Quick Peach Pudding, 144
Quick Quaker Barley
  (pearled), *xvi*
Quick Quaker Oats, *xvi*
Quick-Change Cookie (carob
  chip), 164
Quick-Change Cookie (mild
  chocolate), 164
Quick-Change Cookie (plain),
  164

R

raspberries, nutritional
  analysis of, 175
Raspberry Malt, 182
Raspberry Popsicles, 181
Raspberry Tapioca Pudding,
  138
Raspberry-Peach Pie, 104
recipes, reading thoroughly,
  xvii, 4
reduced-acid orange juice
  brand recommendation,
    xv
  and sugar-free baking, *xv*
Rhubarb-Apple Pie, 105

Rhubarb-Strawberry-Apple
  Pie, 106
Rice Circle Cookies (Oil-
  Based), 167-68
Rice Circle Cookies
  (Shortening-Based),
  166-67
Rice Dream Original 1
  percent Fat Non-
  Dairy Beverage, *xvii*
rings
  Holiday Fig- or Date-
    Cinnamon Ring, 37-38
Roasted Sunflower Topping,
  132
rolls
  Apple-Cinnamon Rolls, 23-
    24
  Apple Drizzle Topping, 27
  Apple-Nut Cinnamon Rolls,
    25-26
  Cloverleaf Rolls, 22-23
  Orange Drizzle Topping, 30
  Pear-Cinnamon Rolls, 23-24
  Pineapple-Orange
    Cinnamon Rolls, 28-29

S

salad dressing
  Almond Salad Dressing, 193
  Quick Lettuce Salad
    Dressing, 194
  Salad Dressing with Olive
    Oil, 192
  Sesame Salad Dressing, 191
  See also dips, mayonnaise
Salad Dressing with Olive Oil,
  192
salads
  Egg-Free Potato Salad, 197
  Potato Salad, 196
sauces
  Apple Pudding Sauce, 139
  Apple Sauce, 141
  Fast-and-Easy Fruit Sauce,
    142

214